PROBLEM SOLVING and EDUCATION: ISSUES in TEACHING and RESEARCH

Edited by

D. T. TUMA
Carnegie-Mellon University

F. REIF
University of California, Berkeley

LEA LAWRENCE ERLBAUM ASSOCIATES, PUBLISHERS
1980   Hillsdale, New Jersey
DISTRIBUTED BY THE HALSTED PRESS DIVISION OF
JOHN WILEY & SONS
New York   Toronto   London   Sydney

Lawrence Erlbaum Associates, Inc., Publishers
365 Broadway
Hillsdale, New Jersey 07642

Distributed solely by Halsted Press Division
John Wiley & Sons, Inc., New York

Library of Congress Cataloging in Publication Data

Main entry under title:

Problem solving and education.

   Proceedings of a conference held at Carnegie-Mellon
University, Pittsburgh, Oct. 9-10, 1978.
   Bibliography: p.
   Includes indexes.
   1. Problem solving—Congresses. 2. Problem
solving—Study and teaching—Congresses. 3. Curriculum
planning—Congresses. 4. Research—Congresses.
I. Tuma, David T. II. Reif, Frederick, 1927–
BF441.P74   370.15′2   79-22461
ISBN 0-470-26918-9

Printed in the United States of America

CONTENTS

Preface

Problem solving is of ubiquitous importance whenever knowledge must be flexibly used (i.e., in any endeavor requiring more than the rote memorization or recall of information). Hence problem solving plays a central role in all the sciences and in most other fields. Furthermore, there is an increasing need to teach improved problem-solving skills to students who must be adequately prepared to cope with a world characterized by growing complexity, rapid change, and vastly expanding knowledge.

Both intellectual and technological developments suggest that the present time is opportune for examining our current knowledge about problem solving and its relevance to practical education. On the intellectual side, recent years have witnessed increasing work devoted to problem solving. Thus researchers in modern cognitive psychology and artificial intelligence have contributed substantially to a basic understanding of the information processing responsible for effective problem solving. Some of these workers have recently also come to address problems sufficiently complex to be germane to practical instruction. In addition, some educators have attempted to teach improved general problem-solving skills, and some have thereby also been led to a greater concern with underlying mechanisms of problem solving. The resulting convergence of interests between pure researchers and applied educators thus makes the time ripe for stimulating better interaction and for examining fruitful directions for further work.

On the technological side, recent advances in electronics are dramatically increasing the power, while decreasing the costs, of computers and other information-processing technology (such as new video technology). As a result, one can expect that the next few years will see such technology become widely available in homes, schools, and offices. If recent insights into problem solving, artificial intelligence, and other cognitive processes can be used effectively, there exists thus an unprecedented opportunity to further significant educational goals through new, widespread information technology.

The preceding reasons motivated us to organize a conference on "Problem Solving and Education: Issues in Teaching and Research." The specific aims of this conference, held at Carnegie-Mellon University in October 1978, were the following: (1) to bring together researchers and educators concerned with problem solving so that they might engage in a mutually beneficial exchange of ideas; (2) to legitimize and encourage the teaching of problem-solving skills in various educational context; and (3) to provide suggestions about practical methods of teaching problem-solving skills and about future research on problem solving.

The conference did succeed in bringing together many of the people most actively interested in problem solving and most knowledgeable about the field. Hence, it seemed beneficial to publish the proceedings of the conference, in order to make its main discussions available to a broader audience. In particular, we hoped that these proceedings would provide a summary of current thinking and relevant literature about problem solving, would reveal some of the existing gaps and difficulties, and would suggest future directions to be explored.

Since problem solving encompasses a vast range of intellectual activities, some attempt was made to limit the scope of problems discussed at the conference and in these proceedings. Thus the emphasis is on problems sufficiently complex to be of realistic practical or educational significance, yet sufficiently simple to be amenable to research on underlying cognitive mechanisms. Nevertheless, the diversity of problems considered is still very large, perhaps excessively so.

The proceedings, following the format of the conference, are subdivided into five parts. Each of these usually includes a few main papers, followed by the remarks of a discussant who provides a broader critical perspective. Part I presents an overview of some recent work on problem solving; Part II discusses some educational implications of research on problem solving; Part III deals more specifically with instruction in problem solving; Part IV points out the needs for complex problem solving in contemporary society; and Part V recapitulates selectively some of the central issues raised in the preceding discussions. The topics discussed in these five parts are, however, not sharply distinct.

One main theme addressed in the papers concerns basic research on problem solving and its relevance to education. James Greeno reviews some recent theoretical work on problem solving. Ira Goldstein, from the perspective of artificial intelligence, discusses the educational implications of computational models of teaching and learning. Herbert Simon, who has done pioneering work on detailed information-processing models of human problem solving, talks about the role of general problem-solving skills in education. Finally, Jill Larkin, emphasizing the particular domain of problem solving in physics, stresses how psychological experimentation and model building can fruitfully interact with concerns for providing effective instruction in problem solving.

The other main theme in the papers concerns practical attempts designed to teach students improved problem-solving skills. Moshe Rubinstein describes his own work in establishing and teaching at a major university an interdisciplinary problem-solving course. Michael Scriven, from the vantage point of philosophy and educational implementation, makes some general remarks about approaches to problem solving that are particularly pertinent to education and real-world problems. Finally, Richard Teare comments on how efforts to teach problem-solving skills are relevant in professional curricula.

The papers of the three discussants (Reif, Norman, and Hayes) all emphasize, from somewhat different points of view, the close interrelation between theoretical work on cognitive processes and applications to practical instruction. Finally, Allen Newell summarizes succinctly some of the crucial issues emerging in all the preceding discussions.

It is our hope that these proceedings may provide a useful perspective about some current work concerned with problem solving. We also hope that they may encourage more people to study problem solving or to devote attention to the teaching of problem-solving skills. If some of these hopes are realized, then another conference in the near future might be able to discuss more specific research findings and more convincingly successful projects effective in teaching widely useful problem-solving skills.

Finally, we wish to express our appreciation to Richard M. Cyert, president of Carnegie-Mellon University, for his encouragement and support, which made it possible to organize this conference and to publish these proceedings.

DAVID T. TUMA
FREDERICK REIF

OVERVIEW

1 Problem Solving and Educational Policy

Richard M. Cyert
Carnegie-Mellon University

The academic area is one of the most difficult areas to change in our society. We continue to use the same methods of instruction, particularly lectures, that have been used for hundreds of years. Little scientific research is done to test new approaches, and little systematic attention is given to the development of new methods. Universities that study many aspects of the world ignore the educational function in which they are engaging and from which a large part of their revenues are earned. The research on problem solving is an extremely interesting and promising development, and its educational implications should be explored in detail. This chapter attempts to explore the need for a greater emphasis on problem solving in the curriculum.

DEVELOPING CURRICULA

We speak knowingly about a curriculum and curriculum problems in higher education without having a general theory to guide us. The liberal arts curriculum must remain merely a series of arbitrary decisions until someone can make a generally accepted definition of an educated person. In professional education, it is generally agreed that the objective is to train problem solvers in particular fields. The physician or lawyer is probably a problem solver. From an information-processing viewpoint, professional education is an attempt to program the individual with several bodies of knowledge. As a problem faces an individual, he or she must be able to retrieve the information necessary to solve the problem and to know how to utilize the retrieved information effectively in order to solve the problem.

This model describes professional education. From an information-processing standpoint, professions are arts rather than sciences. They consist of an information-retrieval system and programs for utilizing the information to solve the problems of the profession. Traditionally in education we have concentrated on the bodies of knowledge in our professional training. We have been, for example, concerned with the fields or disciplines that a prospective business manager should know. We have endless arguments in the process of constructing a curriculum for management over the amount of economics, statistics, or psychology that should be in the curriculum. There is relatively little interest in teaching the student to utilize the information for problem solving. One of the reasons for our concentration on the disciplines that should be taught is that we are knowledgeable about that aspect of education. We can impart information quite effectively. We are much less effective in teaching individuals ways of utilizing this information for the solution of professional problems.

One approach that is used in management education, the case method, concentrates almost completely on the problem-solving aspects but follows the philosophy that the problem solving is a matter of judgment that is developed with practice. The method assumes that the student learns by simulated experience. By seeing the solutions that other students offer, and by discussing one's own solution, it is believed that the student learns how to make better judgments—that is, to solve the problems of management more effectively.

At the other extreme, in management education, are the people who believe that all management problems can be expressed in an analytical form and that the problem-solving methodology consists of learning certain techniques involving mathematics, statistics, and occasionally the computer. For this group, the teaching of problem solving in the curriculum is relatively straightforward.

Curriculum design, however, is more complicated than either of these extreme solutions would seem to make it. Most problems that professionals must face are a mixture of problems requiring analysis, experience, and judgment. It is rare that there is a unique answer to a complicated problem. Thus the process of problem solving is useful to teach, but it is difficult to teach. In the case of most curricula, a good job is not done on teaching the problem-solving aspects of professional life. Usually there are some artificial problems that give the student an opportunity to exercise some of the techniques that he or she has learned, and there are some cases that give the simulated experience we have described. The actual process of functioning as a professional is not well taught in the classroom by these methods. The problem-solving process is one that tends to be learned when the student is on the job and is forced to face real problems and function as a professional.

THE STUDY OF PROBLEM-SOLVING BEHAVIOR

From the standpoint of educational policy, it would be highly desirable to have a way of teaching the problem-solving process. The achievement of that objective is one of the reasons why the work on problem solving is important. To improve education we need a well-developed methodology of problem-solving behavior that would be general—that would be useful for students in all disciplines and professions. It would then be possible to put such a course in the curriculum as preparation for teaching the more specific methods of the particular profession. If the general method were a good one, it should enable the student to learn professional habits more quickly and, hopefully, better.

Reif and his group have attempted some experiments in the teaching of problem-solving skills. The aim of the several experiments has been to determine if it is possible to teach a general problem-solving approach to students and to see whether students with this general problem-solving skill can then learn some specific tasks (such as solving problems in physics or engineering) faster than those students who have not had the general problem-solving teaching. None of the experiments are conclusive enough to show results that are transferable to large numbers. However, the experiments have interesting implications (Larkin & Reif, 1976):

(1) Although the possession of such cognitive skills is essential for effective performance in science courses, our data indicate that many students never acquire these skills adequately through the usual lectures, discussion sections, tests, and problem sets. Furthermore, even if they do, the process whereby they acquire such skills without specific instruction tends to be slow and inefficient.

(2) General cognitive skills necessary for effective performance in science can be taught and should be considered a proper subject for explicit instruction, just as much as the facts and principles ordinarily taught in a science course. (Indeed, it should be possible, as we are now attempting, to teach a special course where such general cognitive skills constitute the primary subject matter.)

(3) Definitive advantages ensue by merely specifying certain general cognitive skills (such as gaining understanding of new relations) as explicit teaching goals for a course: The instructor can then teach deliberately toward this goal. The students are fully aware that they should try to orient their learning toward this goal. Finally, the explicitness of the teaching goal makes it easier to diagnose the students' learning difficulties.

(4) Suppose that a deliberate effort is made to teach students some generally useful learning skills early in a course. Then instruction can afterwards be provided with less elaborate teaching materials, since one may take advantage of the fact that students have become more effective and independent learners.

(5) A general learning skill taught to students is likely to be widely useful to them in other courses and in their future careers [p. 439].

These experiments are small and far from conclusive. They are interesting, however, especially since the results relate to physics. Physicists, in particular among the persons in the various disciplines, believe they have their own special methods of problem solving and that a general approach can serve no purpose. These experiments should be extended, and with larger samples more conclusive results may be forthcoming.

APPLY GENERAL PROBLEM SOLVING

Unfortunately, the educator who wishes to utilize the results of current problem-solving research is under a severe handicap. There are no general theorems or laws that one can easily apply. (This comment is not meant as a criticism but rather a lament.) The results that can be drawn are in the form of heuristics. Many of these can be useful. Rubinstein (1975) has done the best job of attempting to draw these together.

1. Total Picture
Before you attempt a solution to a problem, avoid getting lost in detail. Go over the elements of the problem rapidly several times until a pattern or a total picture emerges. Try to get the picture of the forest before you get lost in the trees.

2. Withhold Your Judgment
Do not commit yourself too early to a course of action. You may find it hard to break away from the path, find it may be the wrong one. Search for a number of paths simultaneously and use signs of progress to guide you to the path that appears most plausible.

3. Models
Verbalize, use language to simplify the statement of the problem, write it down. Use mathematical or graphical pictorial models. Use abstract models such as symbols and equations, or use concrete models in the form of objects.

A model is a simpler representation of the real world problem; it is supposed to help you.

4. Change in Representation
Problem solving can also be viewed as a change in representation. The solutions of many problems in algebra and mathematics in general consist of transformations of the given information so as to make the solution, which is obscure, become transparent in a new form of representation. Most mathematical derivations follow this route.

5. Asking the Right Questions
Language in all its forms is a most powerful tool in problem solving. Asking the right question, uttering the correct word, or hearing it, may direct your processing unit to the appropriate region in your long-term storage to retrieve complete blocks of information that will guide you to a successful solution.

6. Will to Doubt

Have a will to doubt. Accept premises as tentative to varying degrees, but be flexible and ready to question their credibility, and, if necessary, pry yourself loose of fixed convictions and reject them. Rejection may take the form of innovation, because to innovate is, psychologically, at least, to overcome or discard the old if not always to reject it outright.

7. Working Backwards

Do not start at the beginning and follow systematically step by step to the end goal.

The solution path is as important as the answer and, in problems where the goal is specified, the path is the solution.

8. Stable Substructures

In complex problems it helps to proceed in a way that permits you to return to your partial solution after interruptions. Stable substructures that do not collapse or disappear when you do not tend to them will serve this purpose.

9. Analogies and Metaphors

Use an analogy whenever you can think of one. An analogy provides a model which serves as a guide to identify the elements of a problem as parts of a more complete structure. It also helps recognize phases as elements of a complete process.

10. Talk

When you are stuck after an intensive effort to solve a problem, it is wise to take a break and do something else. It is also helpful to talk about your problem at various stages in your search for a solution. Talking to someone may help you pry loose of the constraints we mentioned, because your colleague may have a different world view and he may direct you to new avenues of search when he utters a word or asks a question [pp. 14–21].

The practical problem with these heuristics is their unrelatedness. There is no general theory to guide the student as to the order in which to use these heuristics nor any approach that relates the individual heuristic or subsets of them to particular problems. A raw empirical approach must be taken. On the other hand, Rubinstein's book is several years old, and there may be new results that correct this deficiency. Hopefully, this conference attends to this point.

CONCLUSION

Over and above the problem of getting the material in a form in which it can be applied, we have the problem of getting our colleagues to adopt something new. Perhaps the most difficult organization to change in society is the university. Scratch a professor from any discipline and you will receive a lecture on how business organizations, churches, governments, etc., should reform. Yet, universities ignore the problems of education in their own institutions.

The most obvious indication of the strength of the resistance to change is the continued existence of the lecture. In a real sense, the lecture was rendered obsolete with the birth of the book. Yet no professor would ever concede that the lecture is any less important than it ever was in the past. Part of the reason for the continued importance of the lecture is that the lecturer himself receives enjoyment from lecturing. Students do not rebel against the lecture, because the lecturer shows by the subject matter of the lecture the important areas for the course and the examinations. The more fundamental reason for the lack of change in teaching methods is that institutions of higher education have shunned the scientific approach to studying education in their own institutions.

A striking example of missed opportunities lies in the field of learning theory. Psychologists who study cognitive processes have been concerned for some time with attaining a better understanding of the way man learns. At the level of higher education, there is practically no attempt to make use of any of the material from learning theory in their teaching methods. The reason for this lack of utilization is clear. The psychologists have not attempted to slant their research or their findings toward higher education. Their research has more general objectives. At the same time, faculty members make little or no effort to study learning theory with a view to applying it in their teaching function.

It would obviously be possible to document further the lack of attention paid to the educational process in higher education. The reward system in most high-quality universities gives a heavy weight to research, heavier than to education. A major reason for this state of affairs is the private nature of education in colleges and universities. Academic freedom includes the privacy of the classroom. Research results, on the other hand, are public and are easier to evaluate. It is possible to use a variety of approaches to evaluate teaching, including (but not exclusively) student evaluations. However, only with strong administrative leadership will faculty members give appropriate attention to teaching.

Thus it is fair to say that the problem of effecting the utilization of problem-solving research in the actual educational process is not simple. It is not only the research that has to produce applicable results. The ultimate responsibility for seeing that the revolution is realized lies with those of us responsible for educational policy in our institutions—perhaps an appropriate subject for our next conference.

REFERENCES

Larkin, J., & Reif, F. Analysis and teaching of a general skill for studying scientific text, *Journal of Educational Psychology,* 1976, *68* (4).
Rubinstein, M. F. *Patterns of problem solving,* Englewood Cliffs, N.J.: Prentice-Hall, 1975.

2 Trends in the Theory of Knowledge for Problem Solving

James G. Greeno
University of Pittsburgh

Since the aims of the present conference are practical, but the participants include fundamental research investigators, it seems reasonable to begin by raising the question of what has been learned from fundamental research that has implications for the nature of practical training in problem solving. The answer you receive will depend on which theorist tries to answer, but it seems clear from our preconference summaries that all the theorists on this program believe that substantial findings with important implications have been obtained in fundamental research on problem solving.

My personal characterization of the major contributions of fundamental research on problem solving involves two general points. First, I believe that we have made progress toward a fundamentally new conception of the relationship between problem solving and knowledge. Second, we are developing a more differentiated understanding of the cognitive processes involved in problem solving. These two points involve an interesting contrast. Our increased understanding of the role of knowledge in problem solving has blurred a distinction that was previously thought to be fundamental in defining the nature of problem solving, but our understanding of problem-solving processes has introduced new distinctions in characterizing the domain.

Problem Solving and Knowledge

A few years ago it seemed reasonable to distinguish sharply between performance based on knowledge and performance involving problem solving. Performance based on knowledge was not valued as highly, of course. Phrases such as "*merely* applying an algorithm," or "*just* remembering how to do it," express the generally low opinion of performance in which the knowledge used by the performer is presumed to be understood by the person who is judging the performance. Performance involving problem solving was esteemed more highly, often described as "*real* problem solving," when the person judging the performance was unable to identify a suitable knowledge base for the performance.

One of the consequences of recent fundamental research in problem solving has been a serious erosion of the distinction between knowledge-based performance and problem solving. One cause of this erosion has been our increasing ability to identify the knowledge that is used when someone solves a problem—that is, when someone *really* solves a problem. All problem solving is based on knowledge. A person may not have learned exactly what to do in a specific problem situation, but whatever the person is able to do requires some knowledge, even if that knowledge may be in the form of general strategies for analyzing situations and attempting solutions.

The other reason that the distinction between knowledge-based performance and problem solving has eroded is that we now can characterize the performance of individuals who solve problems; and when we carefully consider the performance that occurs in more routine situations, we find that the essential characteristics of real problem solving are there also. Consider the following example: Find the indefinite integral,

$$\int \frac{e^{2x} \, dx}{3 + 4e^{2x}}. \tag{1}$$

The solution is obtained by applying a simple formula,

$$\int \frac{du}{u} = \ln u + C, \tag{2}$$

with $u = 3 + 4e^{2x}$. Of course, a small change is required in the numerator: $du = 8e^{2x} \, dx$, not $e^{2x} \, dx$. But this is easily accomplished by multiplying and dividing by 8, leading to the answer: $1/8 \ln(3 + 4e^{2x})$.

Although we usually do not consider solving simple calculus exercises as problem solving, the important characteristics of problem-solving performance are present in the process. A subgoal is formed to transform the expression into the form du/u, and a problem-solving operator is applied to achieve that subgoal. When that has been achieved, the main plan of solving the problem with Eq. (2) is carried out.

For those who might find this exercise too simple to merit the attribution of problem solving, consider a slightly more complex case: Find

$$\int \frac{e^{2x}\,dx}{2e^x + 1}. \tag{3}$$

This is solved with the same plan as Eq. (1), but there is a difficulty. If $u = 2e^x + 1$, then

$$\frac{du}{u} = \frac{2e^x\,dx}{2e^x + 1}, \tag{4}$$

and when we try to transform the initial expression, we arrive at

$$\int \frac{e^x}{2} \cdot \frac{2e^x\,dx}{2e^x + 1}. \tag{5}$$

It's not clear that there is any rational way to proceed with this, but a solution can be obtained if we set aside the goal of reducing differences between the existing and desired expressions. The term e^x won't go away, but we can alter the part of the expression that is already in the form that we want it:

$$\frac{2e^x}{2e^x + 1} = \frac{2e^x + 1 - 1}{2e^x + 1} = 1 - \frac{1}{2e^x + 1}, \tag{6}$$

and this leads (rather miraculously) to

$$\int \frac{e^x}{2} \left[1 - \frac{1}{2e^x + 1} \right] dx = \int \frac{e^x\,dx}{2} - \int \frac{e^x\,dx}{2(2e^x + 1)}, \tag{7}$$

which is solved easily.

The contrast between these two exercises is meant to illustrate a disturbing possibility. We have a tendency to think of Eq. (3) as a stronger example of problem solving than Eq. (1), because the algorithm for solving problems of this kind cannot be applied directly, and the problem solver must engage in some nontrivial search for a solution. However, there is a potential conflict between this view of problem solving and good pedagogy. I happen to think that exercises like (3) are counterproductive both for learning mathematics and for learning most aspects of problem solving. The problem is solved by an artifical trick rather than by application of any general principle that clarifies or enriches any mathematical content. At best, exercises like (3) reinforce the response of exploring a problem space when one's available algorithms lead to dead ends. Unfortunately, they also reinforce the impression that solutions of "real" problems depend on luck or revelation rather than on knowledge, skill, or other factors that the student might hope to acquire with diligent study and practice.

I hope that I've persuaded you that the need to search in equation (3) does *not* necessarily make it a more interesting or pedagogically useful problem than the simpler Eq. (1), to which we return to consider the processes that are required for its solution. The solution requires planning at least in Sacerdoti's (1977) sense of choosing a global action that is instantiated in the specific problem situation. A process of understanding is required; in order to select the correct plan, the problem solver must recognize that the problem has general features that correspond to preconditions of the plan. However, other features that are needed are not present, and that leads to setting a subgoal of transforming the expression so it conforms to the preconditions of detail.

The point of this part of my discussion is to illustrate that the major cognitive components of problem solving turn out to be present in many situations in which we are not accustomed to honoring successful performance as instances of problem solving. It is certainly important to distinguish between: (1) situations in which the performer has relatively specific knowledge that makes problem solving quite easy; and (2) other situations in which the performer must resort to more general knowledge and procedures to solve a problem. However, the specificity of available knowledge is a matter of degree, not kind. It is seriously misleading to label performance in some situations as problem solving and in other situations in which the same kinds of cognitive processes occur as not involving problem solving. A continuum should be called a continuum, not a dichotomy.

The argument against dichotomizing performances into a category that includes problem solving and a category that doesn't is no mere theoretical technicality. It strongly determines what kinds of credit we give students for the things they learn how to do, and the kinds of credit we give teachers for the things they successfully teach to students. The belief that problem solving occurs only when a person lacks critical knowledge about the problem has put us in a position like that of a man who is digging a hole and never gets it deep enough because, no matter how far he digs, he is still standing on the bottom. If a student has learned whatever knowledge is required for solving a problem, then the student can't get credit for problem solving, because the student merely is applying the knowledge that (s)he has been taught. Of course, if a student lacks the knowledge needed to solve a problem, the student won't be able to solve it. On this analysis, students are bound to be poor problem solvers, because the only way they can be good problem solvers is by doing things they haven't learned how to do. As soon as we teach them how to solve a class of problems, we take away the credit they ought to be getting for doing it successfully.

I maintain, contrary to popular belief, that students are remarkably successful in solving problems, and that our present instructional system is extremely successful in teaching students how to solve problems. I suggest that the widely held opinion to the contrary is both mistaken and pernicious and will be corrected as soon as people come to realize that significant processes such as understanding, planning, and organizing activity by setting subgoals are very much present in a great many activities that students learn to accomplish routinely. These routine activities, therefore, ought to be counted for what they are—namely, as perfectly legitimate acts of problem solving.

Of course, there are many situations in which we wish that students could learn to solve problems more successfully. There is a rather clear general guideline that emerges from the recent research that I have been talking about. The advice is simply this: To teach students how to solve a class of problems, first analyze the knowledg that they need in order to solve that class of problems, and then carry out instruction that will result in their acquisition of the required knowledge. I think there generally will not be a unique set of knowledge structures that have to be provided for a specified set of problems, and the alternative knowledge structures provide important options in the design of instruction. For example, we often have the option of teaching concepts and procedures that are specifically applicable to quite limited sets of problems, or concepts and procedures that have more general applicability. It is probably the case that specific instruction has the advantage of resulting in successful performance on the kinds of problems used in instruction, but more general concepts and procedures might lead to greater transfer, at least by those students who are able to discover how to apply the general knowledge to new situations. But we need to recognize the necessity of having relevant knowledge if a problem is to be solved.

Varieties of Problem-Solving Skills

If we are to carry out this kind of program involving analysis of knowledge to provide a basis for instruction, it will be helpful to be able to characterize the various kinds of knowledge required in solving various kinds of problems. This brings me to the second main part of this paper, the part involving increased conceptual differentiation in our understanding of problem solving. An analysis that I carried out a few years ago (Greeno, 1978) led me to conclude that there is not a single homogeneous set of skills that we can identify as the important skills of problem solving. The situation is somewhat too complicated for that—different kinds of problems appear to require rather different kinds of skills. On the other hand, it does seem possible to identify some relatively broad classes of problems in which solutions require similar kinds of problem-solving processes and from which we can infer some relatively broad dimensions of problem-solving skill.

The framework that emerged when I examined the psychological literature on problem solving has the form of a typology rather than a taxonomy. The major types of problems that I proposed are problems of: (1) arrangement; (2) transformation; and (3) induction. The reason that these do not provide a taxonomy of problem categories is that many kinds of problems involve combinations of the different types. I think it is useful to think of a three-dimensional space, with coordinates corresponding to the three types of problems: arrangement, transformation, and induction. Then specific problems or kinds of problems can be located in the space in the usual way. Problems that are relatively pure cases of one of the types are near the axis for that type. Problems that present combinations of two or all three of the types of problem requirement are located with large coordinates on the dimensions corresponding to the components that are involved.

I expect that all of the participants in this conference are familiar with the analyses that Newell and Simon presented in *Human Problem Solving* (1972), so I'll refer to those in illustrating the organizing concepts in this proposal. The three problems that Newell and Simon analyzed were cryptarithmetic, simple logic exercises, and choice of a move in chess.

Cryptarithmetic is primarily a problem of arrangement. Several objects are presented to the problem solver, who is required to find an arrangement of the objects that satisfies some stated requirements. For example, in solving DONALD + GERALD = ROBERT, the elements to be arranged are the numbers 0–9, and the arrangement that is required is a set of substitutions of numbers for letters that makes the problem a correct addition. Another example of arrangement problems is an anagram, where a set of letters is to be arranged to form a word. There is a considerable literature of psychological analysis of anagram solution. That literature, consistent with Newell and Simon's analysis of cryptarithmetic, suggests that skill in arrangement problems involves fluency in generating partial solutions along with knowledge of constraints on solutions and ability to use constraints to limit search. The importance of knowledge of constraints was illustrated in cryptarithmetic by differences between problem spaces used by different subjects, with more successful subjects making use of features such as the parity of a sum that was required by earlier choices in the problem.

Logic exercises illustrate problems of transformation, where an initial situation is to be modified to create a goal situation, using a limited set of problem operators. Other familiar examples are puzzles such as the Tower of Hanoi and transportation problems such as Missionaries and Cannibals. Newell and Simon's analysis of logic exercises was based on the process of means–end analysis, and empirical studies (e.g., Jeffries, Polson, Razran, & Atwood, 1977) have supported the suggestion that important skills for solving transformation problems include analysis of differences between the situation that exists in a problem and the problem goal and selection of problem-solving operators that will reduce the differences that are found.

Recent analyses (Fahlman, 1974; Simon, 1975) have shown that means–end analysis can be facilitated by knowledge of sophisticated perceptual concepts that identify relevant combinations of features of problem situations and by knowledge of complex operations that correspond to sequences of problem-solving operators.

Simple examples of induction problems include analogy problems and series extrapolation. Theoretical analyses (Simon & Kotovsky, 1963) as well as empirical studies (Holzman, Glaser, & Pellegrino, 1976; Kotovsky & Simon, 1973) indicate that skill in solving induction problems depends on ability to apprehend relations among problem elements and to integrate them into pattern structures.

Many problems involve combinations of the requirements of different types of problems. Selection of a move in chess probably involves all three of the types of problem requirements. Successful play involves: (1) seeing a way in which the pieces could be rearranged to provide an advantage for one's self; and (2) finding a sequence of moves that will transform the present situation to achieve that advantage. The well-documented ability of skilled players to identify patterns of chess pieces (Chase & Simon, 1973) indicates that the appreciation and use of constraints as well as the formulation of sequences of moves probably are facilitated by the ability to identify structural relationships in the game situation.

There have been two important developments in the analysis of problem solving since I carried out the analysis leading to the typology that I've reviewed briefly here. There has been a significant development of the concept of planning in problem solving. There also has been a substantial beginning of the analysis of processes of representing problem situations, and of the role that representation plays in the problem-solving process.

Planning. A process of planning was considered in some detail by Newell and Simon, but a considerable further development of the idea has been given by Sacerdoti (1977) and by Miller and Goldstein (1976). Sacerdoti's analysis involved a study of the organization of knowledge about actions at various levels in the form of a procedural network. Each action that is included in the system's knowledge structure is known to have a set of preconditions and a set of consequences, as well as a set of component subactions that are performed in order for the action to be accomplished. This organization permits formation of a plan, beginning with a sequence of global actions and proceeding to more detailed components. Miller and Goldstein's study provides important information about interactions between global and local processing in planning. They identified alternating phases of planning and debugging in the solution of simple programming problems.

These analyses raise some rather intriguing conceptual issues about what we mean by planning in problem solving. Miller and Goldstein's analysis is reminiscent of Newell and Simon's analysis of episodes in problem-solving protocols. The various subgoals that a subject identifies and works on provide a useful basis for partitioning the process of solving a problem into constituents. The process of decomposing a problem into manageable subgoals is clearly an important aspect of planning in problem solving. Sacerdoti's analysis is concerned with this process, and his top–down planning system is based on a knowledge structure that permits subgoals to be chosen and placed in an efficient sequence.

The conceptual issue about the nature of planning is raised by Sacerdoti's analysis, because his system generates a plan from prestored knowledge that is specific to the problem domain. For example, NOAH's success in planning the sequence of actions needed to paint a ladder and paint a ceiling (it discerns that the ceiling should be painted first) depends on its knowledge that if an object has just been painted it becomes unavailable for use as an instrument. In NOAH, the process of planning comes to look very much like a process of arranging a set of objects in an appropriate sequence, which is just another kind of problem solving. Of course, NOAH is suspect as a planner just because it is an expert in the problem domain. It already knows the components of action that are needed to solve the various kinds of problems that arise, and this knowledge permits it to avoid the uncertainties that accompany problem solving by systems with less knowledge about the domain.

I think that we have to conclude that planning, like problem solving, is not the kind of process that either does or does not occur in a situation. Instead, it probably occurs in different ways, depending on the knowledge that the problem solver has about the domain. If a person has a rich and well-organized structure of knowledge about actions in the domain, planning seems to occur as a routine form of problem solving similar to that found in ordinary problems of arrangement such as cryptarithmetic or anagrams. Planning by a novice may be more generative, but it seems likely that if a person wishes to become skilled in the kinds of problem solving that anticipate difficulties that can arise in a domain, the acquisition of a well-organized procedural network for the domain may be more useful than the acquisition of general planning procedures.

Representation. The second general issue that has been developed substantially in recent analyses is the issue of problem representation. Earlier analyses of the process of understanding written problems considered the process as a translation from text to a set of problem-solving operators in a problem space (Bobrow, 1968; Hayes & Simon, 1974). More recent analyses, mainly of problem solving in physics, have emphasized processes of understanding that form abstract structures of information that mediate between the text and problem-solving procedures (de Kleer, 1975;

McDermott & Larkin, 1978; Novak, 1976; Reif, in press; Simon & Simon, 1978). The gist of the idea is that in understanding the situation that is described in a problem, the problem solver apprehends relationships that permit selection of subgoals and problem-solving methods by relatively direct retrieval rather than by elaborate search. An example is de Kleer's model NEWTON, in which information in dynamics problems is represented in a qualitative form that simulates envisionment of the problem situation. In imagining the path of an object moving along a surface, ambiguities are generated. For example, if a block is made to slide along the surface of a table, qualitative knowledge is insufficient to determine whether it will reach the edge of the table and fall off or will stop before the edge is reached. The system has clusters of formulas that are used to resolve ambiguities of this kind and eventually to find the answer to the problem. The major function of the representation in NEWTON is to greatly reduce the amount of search that is needed to find relevant problem-solving operators, and empirical observations are consistent with the idea that, in comparison to novices, expert problem solvers are both more skilled in forming abstract representations and require less search in solving physics problems (Larkin, 1977; Simon & Simon, 1978).

The analysis of physics problem solving is leading toward a more powerful theory of understanding in problem solving. Understanding is yet another process that occurs in different ways and to different degrees. We generally hope that students are able to solve problems with understanding rather than mechnically (e.g., Wertheimer, 1945/1959). Furthermore, analyses and data are now confirming the long-standing intuition that understanding is an important facilitating factor in problem solving. Knowledge used in understanding and representing problems apparently simplifies problem solving, reducing the search that is needed to find a sequence of transformations that leads to the goal.

Theoretical Implications.   The analyses of planning and representation that have been developing over the last few years provide a kind of test for the framework that I sketched earlier. It seemed to me, given my understanding of the literature a few years ago, that the main processes involved in solving problems could be characterized as means–end analysis for transformations to achieve a goal, constructive search for a constrained arrangement, and understanding to apprehend the structure of a set of objects. Analyses of planning and representation have been consistent with that general idea. I believe it is reasonable to interpret planning as a process of finding an arrangement of component actions that satisfy constraints such as sequential compatibility. This puts planning in the category of constructive search processes. It seems very reasonable to interpret problem representation as a process of forming a cognitive structure that includes the important relationships among problem components. This puts problem representation in the category of understanding processes.

On the other hand, another aspect of my analysis is weakened by the results of the analyses that have been contributed in recent years. I developed that framework as a typology of problems, and I attempted to identify the main kinds of processes required for solving the various kinds of problems for which psychological analyses had been given. That kind of analysis presupposes that categories of processes and problems are related in a relatively simple way, and the analyses of planning and representation show that that relationship is much more subtle that I had thought. The problems that have been used in these analyses are primarily problems of transformation and thus require skill in means–end analysis, according to the scheme that I presented. However, Sacerdoti's analysis shows that: (1) if a person has the right kind of knowledge for planning, the main solution process becomes one of finding an appropriate arrangement of action components; and (2) the problem requires constructive search rather than means–end analysis. de Kleer's and McDermott and Larkin's analyses show that with the right kind of knowledge for representation, the main solution process becomes one of apprehending the structure of relations in the problem; the problem requires understanding rather than means–end analysis. As with other issues in the theory of problem solving, the issue of the kind of process required for a problem cannot be answered by analyzing only the characteristics of the problem. The kind of process used in solving a kind of problem depends both on the characteristics of the problem and on the knowledge of the problem solver.

Implications for Instruction.   This conclusion has an implication for our prospects for developing a rational technology for instruction in general problem-solving skills. If there were a simple mapping of problems onto general process categories, it would be reasonable to identify the processes required for a class of problems and to try to improve students' capabilities for those general processes. There would be serious theoretical and practical problems involved in that program, but if it worked it could improve students' performance on the target problems, as well as on other problems that involved those skills. The difficulty is that, complex as that program might have seemed 4 or 5 years ago, the results of analyses provided in the meantime have complicated it even more. At least if we accept the cognitive processes of means–end analysis, constructive search, and understanding that I still believe are reasonable, it now seems reasonable to conjecture that solution of all kinds of problems can be facilitated by strengthening appropriate forms of the general processes. It may still be possible to instruct students so that problem-solving processes are strengthened at a general level, but the nature of that instruction and the way in which its effects could be evaluated seem somewhat less clear and more diffuse to me now than they did a few years ago.

It has always been easier to think of ways to give students knowledge relevant to specific kinds of problems than to provide a convincing rationale for instruction intended to strengthen general intellectual skills. I think that recent analyses of planning and representation have increased this discrepancy. With our earlier, simpler view that we could identify the processes required for solving a class of problems, we could hope to provide instruction in those processes and, when we succeeded, to go on to other classes of problems. The picture that is emerging may make it impossible to define the goals of instruction in such a clear way. We might identify the processes of means–end analysis needed to solve a class of transformation problems and instruct students in those. However, we would probably find that students could solve those problems more efficiently if we taught them appropriate planning procedures, involving use of constraints that were not explicitly taught in the context of means–end analysis. If we could accomplish that, we would probably try to strengthen their skills in representing problem situations with relevant abstract schemata.

From one point of view, this prospect is a very positive one, because I think it can allow us to escape from the situation that I talked about at the beginning of this chapter. We don't give students very much credit for the intellectual achievements that they accomplish routinely when they work exercises, and we don't give teachers much credit for teaching them those skills, even though on any of our standard analyses these tasks require serious problem-solving skills. I think the reason that instruction and performance on problems in a specific domain have gotten bad names may be that we have not had a sufficiently developed theory about processes such as planning and representation that are involved in good problem solving, even in specific domains. With the development of appropriate theories about these processes, it should become possible to focus more attention on them, and this could lead both to a better appreciation of students' and teachers' accomplishments and to more effective instruction in the higher forms of problem-solving performance.

On the other hand, there is a discouraging prospect implied by our recognition that problem solving in any domain probably involves a complex combination of all the kinds of cognitive skills that we understand. When we recognize the potential importance of processes such as planning and representation in a domain, we should probably consider ways to instruct students so they can perform those processes more ably. Although this might lead to more efficient instruction, it seems more likely that if we try to teach students more, it will take more time. Predictions about technology should not be taken seriously, but my personal impression now is that as we learn more about the cognitive processes involved in problem solving, the immediate implications of those insights for instruction will involve suggestions for teaching students more about problem-solving in specific domains rather than about problem solving in general. I think that we are likely to find better and better ways of teaching students more and more about less and less. Whereas I believe that this would not necessarily be a bad outcome, I think that many persons find specialization unpleasant, and I think we may be heading toward a situation in which the conflict between specialized skill and general ability is clearer and more troublesome than it is now.

Structure of Problems

One possible response to this view is based on a distinction in the theory of problem solving between well-structured and ill-structured problems. There is a persistent view that the processes of problem solving that we have been able to characterize in reasonably rigorous theories only occur in a limited class of problems that have definite structure, and that the real target for instruction in problem solving involves problems in which definite structure is lacking. If there were fundamental differences between the cognitive processes involved in solving well-structured and ill-structured problems, then it would be reasonable to ignore the kinds of arguments that I have been presenting, at least regarding attempts to strengthen students' skills in situations in which specified problem spaces and definite goals are not provided for them.

Unfortunately for this view, there is evidence that the processes needed for solving ill-structured problems are not different in kind from those involved in solving well-structured problems. This evidence has come from analyses of problem solving in geometry. These problems are quite well structured, but their solutions include processes that seem to have the characteristics needed to account for solution of ill-structured problems. One aspect of ill-structured problem solving is the need to add materials in the problem space. This requirement occurs in a simple form in geometry problems that require constructions, and solution of those problems seems to be dependent on knowledge organized in the way that Sacerdoti (1977) proposed. Planning knowledge, including procedures for identifying missing components of preconditions needed for executing plans, permits an individual to identify auxiliary problems that provide a context for developing new materials needed for solution of the original problem. Another aspect of ill-structured problem solving is the absence of definitely specified goals. This requirement occurs in simple form in geometry problems in which the goal can be achieved in a number of alternative ways. Performance of human problem solvers can be explained by postulating that the problem representation includes a goal structure in the form of a pattern recognition system rather than simply in the form of an object or set of features that must be produced.

Of course, the issue of ill-structured problems will not be settled until we have some relatively complete analyses of problem solving in some genuinely ill-structured problems. Some analyses of ill-structured problem solving are in progress (e.g., Flower & Hayes, in press; Reitman & Wilcox, 1976), and I am optimistic about the continuity of principles between well-structured and ill-structured problem solving that seem to be emerging from these analyses, although we need more complete results before making any definitive judgments.

However, if we are willing to extrapolate from present results, we arrive at the conclusion that ill-structured problem solving depends on the same general kinds of knowledge as we are finding to be the basis of well-structured problem solving. This is discouraging for attempts to increase desirable traits such as creativity and problem analysis in ways that are independent of the content of specific problem domains. I think there are empirical and theoretical reasons for believing that the kind of planning knowledge needed to solve problems, when complete problem spaces or definite goal specifications are not provided, includes knowledge of patterns of objects in the problem domain. I think it is not an accident that most of the creative achievements that we recognize are accomplished by individuals who have spent many years working on problems in the fields in which they make their contributions. There will undoubtedly continue to be exceptional novices who miraculously achieve insights that have been missed by all the experts in the establishment. However, I think there is no basis in current scientific knowledge for changing our present policy of intensive disciplined training for individuals who aspire to making creative changes in the domains in which they choose to work.

A Final Remark

Of course, theorists are notoriously skeptical about the prospects for radical technological change, and we are all familiar with examples of impossible achievements that have been accomplished by inventors who declined to be discouraged by intellectual arguments. Aspiring inventors in the domain of cognition should be especially contemptuous of theoretical discouragement; after all, we have no explanation of how children learn arithmetic, or of how people are sometimes able to resolve disputes by negotiation, or of how it is possible to perform a Chopin etude, much less how it was possible to compose one. If someone is able to teach students how to be better problem solvers, that too is an important achievement that we do not understand adequately. I hope that efforts to develop that technology turn out to be more successful than we can expect them to be with our present knowledge and understanding. It may not be too many years before the state of our science develops to a point where we will know enough to address the question of how general problem-solving skills are acquired. It would be very nice if at that time there were a good supply of instructional programs that were demonstrably successful in strengthening students' general problem-solving skills, because these would provide theorists with good examples for study and analysis.

REFERENCES

Bobrow, D. G. Natural language input for a computer problem-solving system. In M. Minsky (Ed.), *Semantic information processing*. Cambridge, Mass.: MIT Press, 1968.

Chase, W. G., & Simon, H. A. Perception in chess. *Cognitive Psychology*, 1973, *4*, 55–81.

de Kleer, J. *Qualitative and quantitative knowledge in classical mechanics* (Tech. Rep. AI-TR-352). Cambridge, Mass.: Artificial Intelligence Laboratory, Massachusetts Institute of Technology, December 1975.

Fahlman, S. E. A planning system for robot construction tasks. *Artificial Intelligence*, 1974, *5*, 1–49.

Flower, L., & Hayes, J. R. Plans that guide the composing process. In C. Frederiksen, M. Whiteman & J. Dominic (Eds.), *Writing: The nature, development and teaching of written communication*. Hillsdale, N.J.: Lawrence Erlbaum Associates, in press.

Greeno, J. G. Natures of problem-solving abilities. In W. K. Estes (Ed.), *Handbook of learning and cognitive processes*, Vol. 5. Hillsdale, N.J.: Lawrence Erlbaum Associates, 1978.

Hayes, J. R., & Simon, H. A. Understanding written problem instructions. In L. W. Gregg (Ed.), *Knowledge and cognition*. Hillsdale, N.J.: Lawrence Erlbaum Associates, 1974.

Holzman, T. G., Glaser, R., & Pellegrino, J. W. Process training derived from a computer simulation theory. *Memory and Cognition*, 1976, *4*, 349–356.

Jeffries, R., Polson, P. G., Razran, L., & Atwood, M. E. A process model for missionaries–cannibals and other river-crossing problems. *Cognitive Psychology*, 1977, *9*, 412–440.

Kotovsky, K., & Simon, H. A. Empirical tests of a theory of human acquisition of concepts for sequential events. *Cognitive Psychology*, 1973, *4*, 399–424.

Larkin, J. H. *Skilled problem solving in physics: A hierarchical planning model*. Unpublished manuscript, University of California at Berkeley, September 1977.

McDermott, J., & Larkin, J. H. *Re-representing textbook physics problems*. Proceedings of the Second National Conference, Canadian Society for Computational Studies of Intelligence, University of Toronto, August 1978.

Miller, M. L., & Goldstein, I. P. *Parsing protocols using problem solving grammars* (Memo 385), Cambridge, Mass.: Artificial Intelligence Laboratory, Massachusetts Institute of Technology, 1976.

Newell, A., & Simon, H. A. *Human problem solving*. Englewood Cliffs, N.J.: Prentice-Hall, 1972.

Novak, G. S., Jr. *Computer understanding of physics problems stated in natural language* (Tech. Rep. NL-30). Austin, Tex.: Dept. of Computer Science, University of Texas, 1976.

Reif, F. Problem solving in physics or engineering: Human information processing and some teaching suggestions. To be published in a monograph on *Problem Solving* by the American Society for Engineering Education, in press.

Reitman, W., & Wilcox, B. *A program for playing Go: Interim report*. Ann Arbor: University of Michigan, 1976.

Sacerdoti, E. D. *A structure for plans and behavior*. New York: Elsevier, 1977.

Simon, H. A. The functional equivalence of problem solving skills. *Cognitive Psychology*, 1975, 7, 268–288.

Simon, H. A., & Kotovsky, K. Human acquisition of concepts for sequential patterns. *Psychological Review*, 1963, 70, 534–546.

Simon, D. P., & Simon, H. A. Individual differences in solving physics problems. In R. Seigler (Ed.), *Children's thinking: What develops?* Hillsdale, N.J.: Lawrence Erlbaum Associates, 1978.

Wertheimer, M. *Productive thinking*. New York: Harper & Row, 1945. (Enlarged edition, 1959.)

3

A Decade of Experience in Teaching an Interdisciplinary Problem-Solving Course

Moshe F. Rubinstein
University of California, Los Angeles

INTRODUCTION AND BRIEF HISTORY

Ten years ago, the Engineering Concepts Curriculum Projects developed a course entitled "The Man-Made World," with support from the National Science Foundation. The course content was encapsulated in the publication of the book "The Man-Made World" (McGraw-Hill, 1968). According to E. E. David, Jr., and J. G. Truxal, who participated in the projects and wrote the preface to the book: "The course was intended as part of the cultural curriculum, a course for all citizens who will take part in guiding the currents of society." The authors of the book, engineers, scientists, and educators were convinced that the world was rapidly and increasingly shaped by technical accomplishments, and, therefore, it was necessary to make students and citizens in general, more literate about technology.

About the same time, Chauncey Starr, Dean of the School of Engineering, at UCLA, was discussing with me the possibility of developing a campus-wide course that would achieve some of the goals articulated by the Engineering Concepts Curriculum Projects. I studied the possibilities and concluded that a more broad approach was necessary than merely providing literacy about technology and its contributions to shaping our man-made world. I felt that the role of education was to help the learner acquire not only a store of knowledge but also modes of behavior useful in a broad spectrum of situations that might be encountered in a world of rapid change.

In the past, because professions remained unchanged for many years, stored knowledge could be passed on from generation to generation. In the future, high-school and college graduates will have to be retrained more than once in the span of a normal life. In the past, it was common for successive generations to subscribe to the same values. In the future, values may change more than once in a single generation. In an era of rapid social and technological change, education should develop a flexible and unsettled approach to life rather than a false sense of security anchored in a store of knowledge and fixed values. It should strive to cultivate modes of behavior and attitudes useful in a world of constant change. A problem-solving approach to learning, with a focus on process, appeared most compatible with these objectives. Such an approach was to help students transfer what is taught in school to relevant situations outside school by developing the ability to identify problems and to sort out the relevant skills and tools appropriate to deal with them.

The idea was not to develop problem solving as a discipline but rather as a framework for interdisciplinary cooperation. A balance was sought between solution techniques and attributes of human problem solvers, so that problem solving is not reduced to a dogmatic and sterile process. To maintain this balance, human values were to be considered wherever feasible. These attributes were included in the primary objectives of the course that are summarized in the following nine statements:

To develop a general foundation of problem-solving approaches, and master some specific techniques.

To provide a foundation for attitudes and skills productive in dealing with problems in the context of human values.

To emphasize the thinking processes at all stages of the problem-solving activity.

To identify individual problem-solving styles and learn to overcome conceptual blocks and self-imposed constraints.

To expose students to both objective and subjective aspects of problem solving.

To provide a framework for a better appreciation of the role of tools and concepts that the students may have acquired or will acquire.

To bring together students from diverse backgrounds so that they can observe different attitudes and problem-solving styles and learn from each other.

Continued discussions and studies of possible course content and title finally resulted in the development of a course entitled "Patterns of Problem Solving," also known on campus as Engineering 11. In developing the material for this interdisciplinary course, I was influenced by my experiences for more than 10 years as an instructor and director of the UCLA program, "Modern Engineering for Executives." My colleagues in this 6-week summer program, who represented diverse fields of interest, were outstanding scholars and teachers and contributed much to my ability to identifying patterns of problem solving common to all disciplines. Some of these colleagues successfully taught sections of the "Patterns of Problem Solving" course at UCLA.

"Patterns of Problem Solving" was offered for the first time on the UCLA campus in the fall of 1969 to a class of 32 students. By 1973, there were three sections per quarter with an enrollment of 250 students for the year. The yearly enrollment since 1976 has been about 1200 students, with 12 sections of the course each quarter. The course has attracted students from more than 30 major fields and all levels at the University from freshmen to graduate students. Of approximately 3000 students in the course in 1974–1976, about 25% were from each class level, and about 1/3 of the students came from the social sciences. Primary funding for the course comes from the School of Engineering, with additional funding provided by the University Office of Undergraduate Affairs.

Sections of the course have been taught by faculty members and teaching assistants from engineering, management, psychology, law, business, philosophy, architecture, urban planning, mathematics, and computer science. Teaching the course has proven to be an outstanding arena for faculty development. Most of the instructors in the course have been teaching assistants, who are normally Ph.D. candidates, and who undergo special training before teaching the course.

In the fall of 1978, "Patterns of Problem Solving" began its tenth year on the UCLA campus. The course has reached a certain level of maturity in terms of objectives, content, and conduct, but it still retains a measure of flexibility to permit change and growth as new instructors and students from different fields continue to bring new ideas and experiences to the course.

THE COURSE OBJECTIVES AND CONTENT

"Patterns of Problem Solving" was conceived as a course that would serve to integrate skills and attitudes for improving the creative problem-solving abilities of the learner. By concentrating on the thinking process at all stages of problem-solving activity, students were to become aware of their own problem-solving styles, learn to identify strengths and weaknesses, and gain new insights.

The emphasis on the process, and not merely information or results, is stressed at all times—in dealing with simple puzzles or complex social problems. This is best illustrated by a report of a student who was trying to solve the problem of Fig. 3.1, in which two black and two white knights are positioned as shown. The objective is to trade their positions in a minimum number of moves. The constraints are that a square can be occupied by one

FIG. 3.1.

knight at a time, and only the nine squares shown in the figure can be used in the moves. The student documented his efforts in writing as follows:

While attempting to solve the problem, an interesting thing happened. I set out initially by moving the knights randomly. After about 30 minutes, this procedure failing to render a solution, I tried a few combinations in which the knights jumped over each other. This went on for about another half an hour until my wife interrupted me and asked what I was doing on the floor with paper clips and pennies. (I have no chess set, the pennies and paper clips took the place of the knights.) By this time, I was very frustrated and I replied, trying to be sarcastic, "I'm playing leapfrog and ring-around-the-rosey!" Ten seconds later, I had solved the problem. For by having the knights jump over each other in one direction (leap-frog) while remaining on the perimeter of the board (ring-around-the-rosey) their positions are eventually reversed and the problem is solved in a systematic and very efficient manner (1 hour vs. 10 seconds)!

This illustrates two insights. One is that it is helpful to verbalize the problem. I might add that it is helpful to verbalize frustrations. The principle is that in the use of spoken words, some "chunk" of pertinent information may be brought from the brain's storage area and help in the solution process. Second, the notion of "change in representation" is used in the above solution. For an hour, I limited myself to the game of chess in my view of the total problem. I guess I'm a good chess player because I succeeded in outwitting myself. In the last 10 seconds, I blasted myself out of this strict representation of the problem. This happenstance allowed me a new freedom of movement in thinking about the problem, and the solution seemed obvious.

The emphasis in presenting the material is on the transfer of what is taught to relevant practical applications. Whenever possible, the transfer of the tools and concepts to various areas of application is made explicit. This is reflected in both classroom and nonclassroom experiences. Students are required to apply the tools they have learned to a problem of their choice. This becomes the class project and normally includes a statement of present state, goal state, alternative solutions, role of values, stipulation of constraints and uncertainties, and articulation of heuristics in the modeling and solution processes. Projects in the past have covered such diverse topics as choosing a major, selecting a career, buying a car, finding a place to live, and designing an educational game. Though most projects are submitted in written form, some are done orally, on film, or through the use of slides.

Until 1973, I remained the sole instructor of the course at UCLA. As I continued to come in contact with students from different fields, I found myself turning more and more into a student rather than teacher. I read books in philosophy, psychology, artificial intelligence, economics, and art. Students would mention a topic and suggest an approach to problem solving that they learned in their fields, and soon I found myself studying their textbooks. Student delighted in sharing with me their experiences and knowledge. Students seldom miss a class when they think they might have an opportunity to teach the teacher. The attendance in the course had a remarkable record of success.

All along, since 1968, I developed notes that were given out to the students to seek their feedback. By the fall of 1973, I had realized that my colleagues with whom I shared my excitement with the course would undertake to teach it only when a syllabus was prepared for the diverse subject matter treated in the course. This led to the development of such a syllabus. In 1975, the syllabus was published under the title *Patterns of Problem Solving* (Prentice-Hall, Englewood Cliffs, N.J.), along with an Instructor and Solutions Manual.

At present, the course material is based primarily on the book. The book consists of 10 chapters. The first five are devoted to general tools and concepts such as guides to problem solving, language and problem representation, use of tree diagrams and flowcharts, probability reasoning, and modeling. The last five chapters discuss more specific topics such as decision models, cybernetic models, and models of human behavior.

The course material attempts to strike a balance between general concepts and specific techniques. But in all cases, areas of application with emphasis on transfer of approaches and techniques to new areas are made as explicit as possible. This is facilitated by the heterogeneous nature of the class. A student majoring in English may recognize the use of a tree diagram as a useful structure before writing a composition, poetry, or limericks. A computer science student may identify for others in the class the use of trees in structured programming with a top–down configuration in which the level of abstraction is highest at the top and lowest at the bottom of the tree. A student of linguistics will identify yet another application of tree diagrams.

We found that through this emphasis of a number of tools with broad application, students have become more aware of the possibilities to transfer knowledge and tools from one area and its peculiar set of conditions to new conditions. Thus, for example, the use of trees to structure probability problems not only improved the ability of students to solve problems in this area but also gave them a tool they could use in structuring problems in areas as diverse as the design of a sculpture, writing a script for a movie, or planning a career.

The first half of the course and text material are suitable for students with limited background in mathematics. The second half is more mathematical. The entire subject matter of the text was not intended to be taught in a 10-week quarter. The subjects taught, and the extent to which they are covered, depend on the instructor's prerogative. However, there is a core of subject matter upon which every instructor focuses. The text is not the only source of subject material. Some topics covered during the quarter are those that an instructor introduces as a result of individual background.

Although the vehicles used to teach problem solving may vary slightly from instructor to instructor, all instructors include the following aspects of problem solving in general:

- tools for problem representation
- models as aids to thinking
- identifying personal problem-solving styles
- learning to overcome conceptual blocks
- dealing with uncertainty
- focusing on the process of problem solving
- decision making, individual and group
- the role of values in problem solving
- the holistic and interdisciplinary nature of human problem solving.

The emphasis in the subject matter and approach is twofold: to expose the student to the wide range of alternative problem-solving techniques, and to enable the student to use these methods in practical applications. A major focus is on breaking mindsets. Too often, the population at a large university, such as UCLA, tends to stratify. This course exposes the humanities student to objective tools such as numerical models, while introducing the student in physical or life sciences to subjective notions, such as values.

THE PEER TEACHING PROGRAM

In 1973, a new element was added to the course by the introduction of a peer teaching program. The diverse nature of the enrollment dictated the need for individual attention in some areas. Peer teachers provided the answer to this need. This also gave the opportunity to exploit the different backgrounds of outstanding students who completed the course and to use them as an additional learning resource. A further benefit was the more extensive feedback between instructor and student. The peer serves as a link between instructor and student—by informing the instructor of concepts that were or were not conveyed well, and by clarifying parts of the lectures to the students.

In the fall quarter of 1974, a controlled experiment was conducted to evaluate the success of the peer program. Each instructor taught two sections, with peer teachers assisting in one of them. It was found that having the peer teachers was very beneficial. But the instructors were devoting much more time to sections with peer teachers, because they had the additional burden of training their peer teachers. This gave impetus to the creation of a peer training program, which was introduced in the summer of 1974. Since that time, peer teachers and teaching assistants who instruct the course go through a 2-week training program each summer. This is an in-depth seminar also attended by a few experienced peers and instructors. The training program serves to reinforce the material and improve teaching techniques. Participants deliver lectures and take part in simulations of experiences they might have as peers and instructors. The training program also affords an opportunity to get better acquainted and develop a greater sense of community.

For the last 4 years, the peer program has stabilized in terms of the number of peers and their duties. Generally, there are two peers per section. The peers grade homework, tests, and projects and occasionally make presentations in the class. The extent of their participation in class depends on the instructor's needs and desires. Peer teachers also put in office hours in the Peer Room, also known as the instruction laboratory of the course. The peer room is centrally located between the two rooms in which the course is taught, to allow for easy and immediate access by the students, peers, and instructors. The room is staffed Monday through Friday from 10 a.m. to 3 p.m., but it is usually occupied continuously from 9 a.m. to 5 p.m. The number of peers and instructors in the room at a given hour range from a minimum of two, to five or six at the peak hours. Usually, the room is also staffed by at least one instructor each hour.

The primary reason for the peer room is to maximize the effectiveness of the peers; it allows peers and instructors to be immediately available to help students from any section. Since peers are knowledgeable about the concepts and problems in the book, they can assist any Engineering 11 student with homework problems or general concepts.

Many students naturally seek out their particular peer or instructor. This results in the creation of a certain "clientele" for the peer. However, many students visit the peer room at hours convenient to them, which may not coincide with those of their peer teacher. Since the room is staffed throughout the day, these students are still able to receive immediate attention.

With the differing backgrounds of the instructors and peers, and various sample problems, projects, and examples that instructors leave in the room, the lab has also become a type of resource center. In the future, the room will house a small library, computer terminal, and game center.

The peer room also functions as a social center to develop in Engineering 11 a "sense of community." It has become a place where students gather not only to discuss "patterns of problem solving" but also to talk over concepts in "organic chemistry" or "legislative politics." People oftem simply come to eat their lunch before a class. The room is also visited by former Engineering 11 students who come back to talk to their old peer or instructor.

Prospective peers are selected from Engineering 11 and Engineering 12 ("Applied Patterns of Problem Solving"—a more advanced course) with instructor recommendation. Mastery of material and general competence are a must, but another very important quality is personality. Peers are trained not only to answer questions but also to ask motivating questions, so that in the process the students learn to help themselves.

THE EXPERIENCE OF LEARNING AND
TEACHING PATTERNS OF PROBLEM SOLVING

Students find the course very enlightening. They appreciate the practical course content and the personal attention. Outstanding students often become very interested in the material and continue to take related courses. Twice a year, the follow-up seminar course, "Applied Patterns of Problem Solving," is offered to a select group of excellent "Patterns of Problem Solving" students. These students are specially invited by their instructors to take the seminar. Students consider it an honor to be invited to participate in the seminar. In this course, more advanced topics are studied, and students conduct in-depth group projects. One group designed a "UCLA GAME," which is used at UCLA's incoming student orientation the introduce the campus and its regulations to newcomers. Another group analyzed the planning, programming, and budgeting system at a Southern California high school. Other topics have included improving the UCLA fraternity and sorority system and forming a small business. Students sometimes continue these projects by taking independent study courses.

Not only outstanding students find the course appealing. Many students who have not been exposed to problem-solving concepts before find them fascinating. One student, for example, worked very hard throughout the quarter attempting to understand concepts that were alien to him. He was very proud to earn a grade of "C" at the end of the class and thanked the instructor for the only course he'd enjoyed at the university! This student was especially aided by the daily availability of help in the course learning laboratory. "Patterns of Problem Solving" may be unique in that both instructors and students consider the course to be a valuable learning experience. This fact is at the very heart of the reasons for the success of the course.

There are many benefits for course instructors. Instructors often share the same offices. They maintain common office hours in the learning laboratory and meet to discuss their experiences in social get-togethers several times a year. The effects of this constant fraternization are manyfold. The instructors develop close personal friendships. They exchange information on the course, based on their own area of expertise; share amusing or frustrating experiences; develop new problems, examination questions, and class examples; and aid each other in some of the more difficult aspects of the course content. They also discuss some of the more philosophical aspects of teaching: the role of the peer teacher, the best ways to make use of student skills, the proper amount of discussion versus lecture, and so on. An informal tradition exists that some aspects of the course content, emphasis, examples, and so on are always changing. Part of this results from the interchange of ideas among the instructors; as new ideas are developed and are successful, they are communicated to the other instructors and adopted. But more than this, the instructors fundamentally believe in one of the bases of the course content: One must maintain an open mind, a will to doubt, and flexibility. They believe that, in a dynamic world, it makes little sense to set one's plans in concrete, especially in a course that purports to teach the skills necessary to solve real-world problems. Furthermore, the instructors are taught, and believe, that all classes are different; courses have personalities just as people do, and one does not treat all classes alike anymore than one would treat all people alike. Oftentimes an instructor will modify teaching technique or course content to accommodate a particular class of students.

Instructors maintain an honest respect for their students. In a sense, this is a necessity, because in a course that covers subjects from psychology to linguistics to physics to engineering, there may be students who know more about some given subject than the instructor.

EXPERIENCES WITH PATTERNS OF
PROBLEM SOLVING OUTSIDE UCLA

Since 1973, the course has been offered as a NSF Chautauqua-type Short Course for College Teachers conducted by the American Association for the Advancement of Science with support from the National Science Foundation. The short course attracted participants with the same diversity of backgrounds and interests as the students in the UCLA course. In 1974, peer teaching was introduced into this short course by enlisting the involvement of outstanding participants from earlier offerings of the course.

The course consisted of two days in the fall and two in the spring semesters, with an interim period devoted to study and an interim project. The peer program was expanded in 1976 to include the participation of 12 adjunct faculty members recruited from the ranks of outstanding participants who have completed the course. Three adjunct faculty members were assigned to each class of 25 participants. The objectives of the short course were announced as follows:

1. to provide a learning experience that crosses boundary lines between disciplines and is useful in traditional fields of endeavor;
2. to provide a foundation for attitudes and skills productive in dealing with complex problems from the representation stage to creative solution in the context of human values; and
3. to present an approach for developing an interdisciplinary program that can serve all students.

As an interim project, participants were asked to apply "Patterns of Problem Solving" to a topic of their choice that was to include a statement of present state, goal state, alternative solutions, role of values, stipulation of constraints and uncertainties, and articulation of heuristics in the modeling and solution processes.

Courses similar to "Patterns of Problem Solving" have been adopted in a number of schools. For example, R. Kadesch, Professor of Physics at the University of Utah, uses "Patterns of Problem Solving" in a course intended to fulfill a core requirement in the university liberal education program. Kadesch used the text in a class of about 50 students for which there were no prerequisites of any kind. He wrote to me saying: "I should like to report how pleased I am with your text, the course itself, and the more than favorable reception of your materials by the students..."

P. Laughlin, Professor of Psychology at the University of Illinois, uses the text "Patterns of Problem Solving" in a course on "The Psychology of Thinking." His class consists of about 75% advanced psychology students and 25% graduate students from various disciplines.

D. Farley uses "Patterns of Problem Solving" as a reference in support of a course on artificial intelligence in Richland, Washington.

S. Bartlett, Professor of Philosophy at St. Louis University, developed a course entitled "Patterns of Problem Solving" based on the UCLA course. Bartlett uses as textbooks *Patterns of Problem Solving*, by Rubinstein, and *Conceptual Blockbusting*, by Adams. He is also making use of a set of 19 ½-hour videotaped lectures on"Patterns of Problem Solving," byMoshe F. Rubinstein, developed by the UCLA Media Center during a 1975 public lecture series. A brief description of these videotapes is included in the Appendix.

The interdisciplinary nature that characterized "Patterns of Problem Solving" from its inception is in evidence in the adoption of the course by interested faculty from physics, psychology, artificial intelligence, philosophy, chemistry, mathematics, management, business, and other fields.

The interest in teaching problem solving continues to grow. Bartlett, who conducted a survey of problem-solving courses in 1976, found more than 30 universities and colleges that offer a problem-solving course.

EVALUATION OF A PROBLEM-SOLVING COURSE

Bartlett, whose problem-solving course is most similar to the UCLA course, conducted an evaluation of his course. He gave an IQ pre- and posttest to the students. The instrument was the California test of Mental Maturity (CTMM), Short Form 1963, Level 5 (mental-age range common to Grade 12, college, and adult). The results he obtained were as follows (reported in a Final Report of Work Supported by the Lilly Endowment):

Language IQ		*Nonlanguage IQ*	*Total IQ*
Pretest			
mean	126.29	120.88	127.94
range	100–138	100–137	115–142
Posttest			
mean	130.64	127.24	133.41
range	119–146	113–139	123–143

In reporting the results, Bartlett makes the following observations:

The above scores relate only to those students present for both the pre- and post-tests. $N = 17$.

In terms of total IQ, 29.4% of the students demonstrated an increase in IQ score of between 10–17 points. 52.94% of the students increased total IQ scores from 7–17 points. (The standard error of measurement for these tests is 5 points; hence, these increases are statistically significant.) A total of 82.4% of the students showed some increase in their total IQ scores.

In terms of language IQ scores, 23.5% of the students demonstrated an increase of 11–19 points. 35.3% showed an increase of 8–19 points.

In terms of non-language IQ scores, 29.4% of the students demonstrated an increase of 13–24 points. 47% showed an increase of 6–24 points.

It is empirically well-established that increases in IQ scores become progressively more difficult to produce the higher the pre-test IQ mean is. In the present case, the average initial total IQ of students in the class was 127.94. *Any* increases in IQ scores beyond the standard error of measurement, given this starting point, were unusual, and were not expected.

The problem-solving class concentrated on problem-solving techniques of specific kinds—e.g., probability reasoning, use of formal representations, modeling, use of flow charts, decision methods, etc. Skills tested for on the CTMM were not emphasized. (Approximately four class meetings, only, were devoted to the types of problems encountered on the CTMM.) It seems reasonable to believe, then, that the increases detected in IQ scores indicate that general problem-solving skills possess a generalization characteristic. In other words, training in general problem-solving skills appears to improve indirectly a student's verbal comprehension, memory, and quantitative reasoning skills of the kind measured on most IQ tests.

It should also be mentioned that the IQ post-test was given during the last week of classes, before final examinations and Christmas vacation. It is well-known that testing at such times frequently can reduce a student's raw score. In this light, the gains observed are rather more surprising.

Improvement in general problem-solving skills was computed as follows:

(post-test score) – (pre-test score) = improvement on a percentile scale

This score, representing relative improvement on a 100 point scale, was then analyzed in terms of the percentage improvement of the post-test increase in relation to the pre-test score.

The mean improvement on a percentile scale was + 30 points. This corresponded to an improvement of 84.5% in relation to pre-test scores. In other words, on the average, students in the problem-solving class improved their general problem-solving skills by 84.5% in relation to their entry skills at the beginning of the semester [p. 30–32].

CONCLUSION

Our decade of experience with "Patterns of Problem Solving" has had a remarkable record of success. The reasons for this success are the course content; the preparation and training of the teaching staff; the varied opportunities for learning; the availability and helpfulness of the staff; the learning laboratory; and the enthusiasm, dedication, and commitment of the instructors and peer teachers. In a recent evaluation of "Patterns of Problem Solving" conducted by the UCLA Office of Research and Evaluation, a majority of the students stated that the course has improved their reasoning skills and that they have applied the tools and the concepts of the course to real-life situations. This corroborates the findings of Bartlett in the evaluation of his course. So far, our assessments of the course at UCLA have been based on evaluation forms and testimonials from students and faculty. This year we plan to begin an ongoing effort to generate empirical evidence of what contribution the course makes to enhance problem-solving abilities. But even without empirical evidence, on the basis of our decade of experience, I have a strong feeling that we have a good beginning in attempting to teach problem solving as an interdisciplinary course.

EPILOGUE

In working with the teaching staff of "Patterns of Problem Solving," I have used a number of guiding principles that have proven helpful to me through many years dedicated to bringing about learning and growth. I am purposely not using the word "teaching" in describing these efforts, because it does not always follow that teaching leads to learning. Here are some of the principles that have worked for me and have given me continued satisfaction in my efforts:

- If you really want your students to learn a concept, give them an opportunity to teach you, the teacher.
- If a group of students is highly motivated and learns well, stay out of their way. Do not teach them; let them teach you.
- Concentrate on a small number of concepts, and dig deeply into their implication in as wide a field as possible.
- Make explicit the connection between knowledge and its application whenever possible.
- Show respect for the learners by preparing for each session.
- Encourage questions. Some questions are so outstanding that they should not be spoiled by an immediate answer; we should take time to ponder them. If this is the case, tell the students.
- Learn the names of your students. This is one of the best ways to motivate them and gain their respect.
- *Do not* tell a class: "We are behind." Your plan might have been unrealistic. Each class is unique.; adapt your plans to the class and you will always be "on schedule," whatever it may be.
- When you explain something, seek feedback by asking: "Did I make myself clear?" This is better than asking: "Did you understand?"
- Do not express doubt about the learner's abilities to learn.

APPENDIX: TITLES OF VIDEOTAPE LECTURES ON PATTERNS OF PROBLEM SOLVING

Video Tape Lectures on
Patterns of Problem Solving
by
Professor Moshe F. Rubinstein

Descriptive Outline Prepared by
Iris Rubinstein (1976)

This descriptive outline is intended as an aid to the viewer by providing key concepts and diagrams.

These tapes are parts of a series of seven lectures on Patterns of Problem Solving given by Professor Rubinstein.

Tape I — Introduction (2 parts)
Anatomy of a problem.
Role of values in problem representation and solution.

Tape II — Guides to Problem Solving (3 parts)
Schools of thought, common difficulties, general precepts as guides to problem solving, problem representation, paths to solution.

Tape III — Language and Communication (2 parts)
The structure of language, communication and natural language, evolution of written language, art and other forms of problem representation.

Tape IV — Uncertainty and the Will to Doubt (3 parts)
The concept of information, its credibility and value, its relevance; plausible and demonstrative reasoning.

Tape V — Models and Modeling (3 parts)
The purpose, validation and classification of models in the natural world and in human affairs; models of history, the universe, the atom, the brain.

Tape VI — Decision Models (4 parts)
Examples: the farmer, doctor, executive.
Decision criteria, decision under conflict, group decisions.

Tape VII — Values and Models of Behavior (2 parts)
Value judgment, social preferences, consensus, examples of values and choice.

Acknowledgment

The video tapes were prepared with support from the Creative Problem Solving Program Director, Professor Marvin Adelson and the Extended Studies Program, Dean Leonard Freedman.

James Stodel, UCLA Media Center, was in charge of production and editing.

4 Theoretical and Educational Concerns With Problem Solving: Bridging the Gaps With Human Cognitive Engineering

Frederick Reif
University of California, Berkeley

In accordance with my official role as discussant, I shall first comment specifically about the preceding papers and some related concerns expressed by members of the audience. Then I shall turn my attention to some broader issues generally relevant to the entire Conference.

COMMENTS ON GREENO'S PAPER

Greeno emphasizes properly that there is no sharp distinction between problem solving and knowledge-based performance. Indeed, any task aiming to attain some goal constitutes a problem, and the solution of any such problem requires appropriate knowledge. Thus problems may range from "solving a simple algebraic equation" to "formulating a fruitful question for scientific investigation."

However, this ubiquity and communality of problem-solving activities should not obscure some significant differences. Thus various kinds of problems may well require different approaches toward their solutions. (For example, an algorithmic solution of an algebra problem may well differ significantly from the approach required for more open-ended problems.) In particular, problems can differ widely in their complexity and their demands on flexibility for coping with diverse situations. Such differences in complexity and needed flexibility can imply qualitative, rather than merely quantitative, differences between types of problems. For example, as problems become more complex and require more knowledge, the selective retrieval of information becomes exponentially more difficult. Hence the solution of complex problems, unlike that of simpler problems, depends crucially on efficient search procedures and forms of knowledge organization. Thus Greeno may well be right in saying that students are quite good problem solvers, as long as they deal with relatively simple problems. But students' problem-solving capabilities are often found to be quite deficient in the case of more complex problems of the kind encountered in college-level science courses.

As Greeno points out, planning and representation are centrally important issues in problem solving. A concern with these fundamental issues is, I believe, likely to be far more fruitful than the mere construction of problem typologies.

[Inadvertently, Greeno's paper provides a nice example of the utility of generally applicable problem-solving heuristics and of the importance of appropriate problem representation. Thus Greeno's illustrative integration problems led me immediately to apply a general heuristic rule that recommends to "simplify the description of any problem by introducing a new symbol to denote a symbolic expression of disturbing complexity." In this case, the application of this heuristic suggests denoting $e^{2x} = y$ in the first of Greeno's problems, and $e^x = y$ in the second problem. When the integrals are described in terms of the variable y, both integration problems become equally simple, and any "tricky" aspects of the second problem disappear.]

In my judgment, Greeno and some other participants at this Conference exaggerate the conflict between generally applicable problem-solving methods and knowledge or problem solving in specific domains. It is more fruitful to emphasize the general utility of structuring knowledge hierarchically. Indeed, by embedding specific knowledge in more generally applicable knowledge, the resulting knowledge can be more easily remembered, retrieved, modified, or flexibly applied for problem solving. Thus I see no reason for Greeno's concern that we may be forced to teach students more and more about less and less. It is far more likely that knowledge about problem solving can be made manageable and effective in the same way as knowledge about a complex scientific field (i.e., by teaching students powerful general concepts and methods, which can then be supplemented by more specialized knowledge in particular domains).

Finally, Greeno's concluding remarks strike me as unduly negative. Not only does he express doubts about the extent of ultimate progress achievable in work on problem solving. He also leaves us with very few specific suggestions about what directions might fruitfully be pursued, either to obtain deeper insights into problem-solving processes or to develop teaching methods for enhancing students' problem-solving skills.

COMMENTS ON RUBINSTEIN'S PAPER

The most significant aspect of Rubinstein's work is that he has created a practical course specifically designed to teach students general problem-solving methods that transcend a particular subject matter or discipline. This course deals with real-world problems and is addressed to students from many diverse fields, ranging from engineering to the humanities.

It is also clear that Rubinstein's dedication and enthusiasm have succeeded in establishing a course that is realistically viable. Thus the course has been taught for about a decade at a major university, has attracted large numbers of students, has involved the active participation of faculty members from diverse disciplines, has evoked very favorable responses, and has even been extended to other universities.

The course has, however, some limitations. Rubinstein's book itself is mainly, in the words of a book reviewer, a "compendium of theory and practice in mathematically based problem-solving systems" of the type encountered in operations analysis. It does *not* emphasize more universally important nonmathematical aspects of problem solving, nor does it draw significantly on recent insights derived from basic work on problem solving. The actual teaching methods used in the course may, of course, supplement these shortcomings of the book. However, these teaching methods are not well explicated and seem to depend largely on the intuitive approaches adopted by various individual instructors in the course.

Moreover, the approach to the course involves a peculiar paradox. On the one hand, Rubinstein's book stresses heavily the importance of objective quantitative methods in problem solving (even in the case of complex problems concerned with values). Furthermore, Rubinstein says that he tries to teach his students the "will to doubt" so that they may avoid being led astray by preconceptions or self-deception. On the other hand, Rubinstein does not seem to have applied these sound precepts to his own course. Thus, despite the passage of nearly a decade, he has not made any objective assessment of the extent to which his course is actually effective in increasing the problem-solving skills of his students. Instead, he has been content to gather testimonials and questionnaires on students' self-perceptions.

The issue here far transcends Rubinstein's particular course. In education, as well as in other fields, testimonials are a notoriously unreliable and potentially misleading source of evidence. (For example, we all know how enthusiastic persons can convincingly propound the virtues of astrology or of certain anticancer drugs, even when such claims are unsupported or contradicted by objective studies.) Hence, anybody who develops a course designed to teach general problem-solving skills ought to practice what he preaches. In other words, he ought to apply good objective problem-solving methods, and standards of assessment similar to those common in good scientific or engineering work, to assess the effectiveness of such a course and the validity of its underlying educational premises.

GAPS IN CURRENT WORK

Let me now expand my previous comments to address some broader issues relevant to the entire Conference. In particular, I shall argue that current approaches to problem solving suffer from some significant gaps that might fruitfully be bridged.

People interested in problem solving, and well-represented by participants at this Conference, can roughly be divided into two types. One type consists of "cognitive scientists" (i.e., persons primarily concerned with cognitive psychology, computer science, or artificial intelligence). The other type consists of "educators" (i.e., persons primarily concerned with practical teaching or instructional development). Despite their common interest in problem solving, these two types of people are separated by major gaps.

Cognitive scientists tend to think analytically and strive to formulate explicit theoretical models. If they are chiefly interested in furthering basic understanding, they carry out detailed experimental tests in order to validate their theoretical models. If their interests are more applied, they deliberately design practical applications on the basis of their models. In short, the approach of the cognitive scientists is similar to good scientific methodology prevalent in the natural sciences or engineering. However, cognitive scientists are usually not concerned with questions of direct educational interest. Thus, in pursuing their quest for basic understanding, cognitive psychologists may justifiably investigate puzzles, games, or other academic problems only remotely relevant to practical education. Similarly, although workers in artificial intelligence may have practical applied interests, their concern is usually primarily with computer implementation rather than with human subjects.

By contrast, educators are directly concerned with realistic teaching endeavors and with human students. However, they usually approach their tasks in intuitive ways, using rules of thumb rather than analytic methods. Nor do they tend to design their instruction on the basis of explicitly formulated theoretical models. Furthermore, their criteria for educational success or validity are often quite fuzzy. Accordingly, their attempts at assessment tend to be impressionistic, anecdotal, or directed at gathering gross statistical data (rather than at making detailed observations useful for elucidating underlying mechanisms of success or failure).

There is thus a wide gap separating the approaches of the cognitive scientists and the educators. Although the existence of this gap is understandable for historical and sociological reasons, the continuing persistence of this gap is deleterious to future progress. Thus work in education and problem solving could profit substantially if this gap were bridged, if people interested in practical education would build upon the insights and methods of the cognitive scientists, and if educators were to adopt modes of analytic thinking and quality standards of the kind prevalent in other sciences.

But the nature of the gap is more profound than the preceding comments indicate. Indeed, I believe that the gap has significant intellectual implications for the kinds of questions addressed within cognitive science itself.

To explain what I mean, let me begin with a few general remarks about cognitive science. The term *cognitive science* has recently come to be applied to a group of related disciplines characterized by a common approach to complex information-processing systems. Basically, this approach emphasizes detailed investigations and explicit theoretical models of mechanisms underlying complex symbolic tasks. As illustrated in Table 4.1, cognitive science may then be subdivided into several domains according to the following dimensions:

1. One subdivision is according to the information processor of interest. Thus the information processor to be studied may be either a computer or a human being.

2. Another subdivision is according to the type of goal pursued in the studies. Thus the goal may be *descriptive* (i.e., "naturalistic" or "purely" scientific), in which case it is to describe and understand theoretically the properties of the information processor of interest. Alternatively, the goal may be *prescriptive* (i.e., aiming toward a more applied science of design or of the "artificial"), in which case it is to design, on the basis of basic understanding, information processors capable of performing effectively various tasks.

Which of these domains are currently being pursued in cognitive science? In the realm of computers, the disciplines of computer science and artificial

TABLE 4.1
Subdivision of Cognitive Science
According to Type of Information-Processing System
and Type of Scientific Goal

	Descriptive	*Prescriptive*
Computer	Computer science	Artificial intelligence
Human	Cognitive psychology	??
		(Human cognitive engineering)

intelligence encompass both the descriptive and prescriptive aspects of information-processing machines. In the realm of human information processors, cognitive psychology, concerned with the descriptive aspects of human cognition, studies experimentally and theoretically the thought processes actually used by people. But what about the last domain concerned with the *prescriptive* aspects of human information processing? Who, using the approach of cognitive science, is systematically interested in studying modes of information processing specifically designed to improve human intellectual performance? Curiously enough, this domain does not even have a name. Indeed, there are rather few people working in it. This undercultivated fourth domain constitutes then a significant gap within current cognitive science.

PROSPECTS OF "HUMAN COGNITIVE ENGINEERING"

This neglected domain of prescriptive human cognitive science might be called "human cognitive engineering" (or "*human* knowledge engineering," if one adapts a term used by Feigenbaum to denote applied work in complex artificial intelligence). Such human cognitive engineering, in the case of human information-processing systems, would explicitly address questions very similar to those addressed by artificial intelligence in the case of computers. Human cognitive engineering would thus take into account the special capabilities and limitations of human cognitive functioning (e.g., highly developed language and pattern recognition capabilities, but significant memory limitations) in order to address questions such as the following: Can one design or invent modes of human information processing that can specifically enhance human cognitive performance? For example, can one design forms of knowledge organization and symbolic representations that facilitate human thought processes? Similarly, can one design humanly useful procedures for enhancing the effectiveness and efficiency of human performance in problem solving or other cognitive tasks? Furthermore, once such explicit models of humanly useful forms of knowledge have been formulated, can one assess their validity by implementing them with human beings and ascertaining experimentally the extent to which predicted improvements in human performance actually do occur?

What would be the potential utility of pursuing systematic investigations in such human cognitive engineering? There are at least three realms of substantial utility:

1. Such investigations would clearly be very useful for education, since most instructional efforts ultimately aim to improve the cognitive

performance of human students. Investigations in human cognitive engineering thus would be both practically useful by providing methods of teaching students more effectively and theoretically useful by providing deeper insights into teaching and learning processes. Furthermore, if education were viewed as a part of human cognitive engineering, there would be fruitful opportunities for mutually beneficial interaction between practical education and more theoretical work in cognitive science.

2. Human cognitive engineering offers the prospects of enhancing human intellectual performance in various practical tasks and professions. Furthermore, the rapidly increasing sophistication and availability of computers make it likely that interactive man–computer systems will increasingly be exploited to deal with complex problems in many domains. But the effective utilization of such combined man–machine systems will require that the information-processing capabilities of the human component be as well understood and designed as those of the computer. Hence, as much attention will need to be devoted to appropriate human cognitive engineering as to the artificial intelligence that assures effective computer performance.

3. Finally, a concern with human cognitive engineering may also have purely scientific benefits. In formulating theoretical models of complex information processing, one is centrally interested in high-level procedures and forms of knowledge organization. Correspondingly, one would then ideally like to test such models on information processors with sophisticated lower-level capabilities (such as well-developed capabilities of natural-language understanding and pattern recognition). Human beings, despite some of their disadvantages as experimental subjects, possess such language and pattern-recognition capabilities to a much greater extent than present-day computers. Thus human cognitive engineering may derive some purely scientific benefits by its attempts to test theoretical information-processing models by implementation with human individuals.

Is it, however, realistic to expect that work in human cognitive engineering might actually be pursued successfully? Let me mention several examples that suggest how work of this kind might be interesting and fruitful.

Our cultural history itself provides many examples of successful inventions in human information processing. Consider, for instance, the development of musical notation (perfected for the most part by the seventeenth century). This was essentially just the discovery of a particular symbolic representation designed to allow human beings to exploit their visual pattern recognition capabilities in order to describe musical notes. The invention of this symbolic representation had, however, enormous implications. It allowed the easy storage and transmission of musical information. It greatly increased the ability to analyze music and thus led to the disciplines of harmony and counterpoint. Most important, it vastly enhanced human capabilities to design complex musical structures. Indeed, without the invention of musical notation, the composition of a Beethoven symphony would have been an impossible task.

A more contemporary example, relevant to problem solving, is provided by the recent development of "structured programming." The origin of this development is the increasing recognition that the main bottleneck in the implementation of complex computer tasks is often not the computer itself but the human trying to solve the problem of designing computer programs. Within the last decade, this recognition led various people (such as E. W. Dijkstra, C. A. R. Hoare, N. Wirth, and others) to analyze systematically the process by which persons might design computer programs more effectively, efficiently, and reliably. This analysis has led to a set of prescriptive precepts that have come to be called *structured programming*. These precepts include procedures of successive refinement by which any program can ultimately be synthesized out of a small set of standardized primitive subunits of optimally small size. The precepts also specify ways of structuring any program hierarchically into modules small enough for easy human processing. Moreover, they suggest symbolic representations (such as indentation schemes on a written page) specially designed to facilitate the human comprehensibility of programs.

Several points are worth noting about the preceding example:

1. Structured programming, although inspired by the existence of computing machines, is really not centrally concerned with computers; rather, it addresses the question of how human beings can effectively solve the problem of writing complex programs (irrespective of whether or not these are ultimately implemented on a computer). Thus the precepts of structured programming are prescriptive and specifically designed to enhance *human* problem solving in a particular domain.

2. These precepts have, in practice, been found to be quite successful and are coming to be increasingly used. Indeed, they provide a generally applicable framework within which one can embed more specific knowledge about particular algorithms or other detailed aspects of computer prgramming.

3. Some of these general precepts are probably equally applicable in problem-solving domains outside of computer science.

As my next example, I mention some work originally inspired by practical educational concerns. This work, carried out by some collaborators and me at Berkeley, has had the general goal of studying human problem solving in a realistically complex domain and then of using the resulting insights to teach students improved problem-solving skills. (In particular, we focused on problem solving in the domain of basic college physics, since this domain is sufficiently simple to offer prospects for progress in basic understanding, yet sufficiently complex to be representative of realistic instructional problems.) What is interesting, although not too surprising, is that this systematic attempt to address educationally relevant concerns has quite naturally led us to identify and study issues that seem to be centrally important to most problem solving and that have also received attention in other areas of cognitive science.

One of these issues is the great power of a problem-solving procedure that proceeds by successive refinements, starting from gross global descriptions of a problem and elaborating these to obtain successively more detailed descriptions. Such a procedure involves planning at various levels (in a manner reminiscent of Sacerdoti's artificial-intelligence work mentioned in Greeno's talk). It also exploits the utility of different symbolic representations to describe the same problem at different levels (e.g., verbal or pictorial representations for global descriptions, and mathematical symbolism for more detailed descriptions). Theoretically, there are good reasons why problem solving by successive refinements is an efficient search method; it rapidly narrows the domain of search by a stepwise procedure involving only a few decisions per step. Experimentally, Jill Larkin's observations (while she was still in Berkeley) showed that the methods actually used by experts and novices solving physics problems differ precisely along this crucial dimension. Thus experts tend to proceed hierarchically by successive refinement, planning problems in qualitative terms before proceeding to mathematical details. On the other hand, novices tend to describe problems at a single detailed level, merely assembling sequentially individual mathematical equations.

Another centrally important issue arising in our work concerns the effective organization of the knowledge used for problem solving. Indeed, we expect that problem solving by a method of successive refinements should be facilitated if the knowledge in a person's mind is organized hierarchically at several levels of detail (with correspondingly different symbolic representations and with the most important information at the top levels). To check the utility of such a form of knowledge organization, my student Bat-Sheva Eylon has recently carried out some experiments to study specifically how the organization of a person's internal knowledge affects his or her performance on various tasks. For example, in one such experiment, the knowledge consisted of an argument typical of the kind presented in mathematics or physics courses. In a well-controlled experiment, we induced a person to incorporate his or her knowledge about this argument in one of two alternate forms: either (1) in the form of a linear sequence of well-justified steps; or (2) hierarchically at two levels (a higher level containing a global description of the argument in a few steps, and a lower level consisting of the detailed elaboration of this high-level argument). The experiment showed clearly that subjects whose knowledge of the argument was organized hierarchically could afterward not only remember the argument significantly better; they could also more easily modify it, generalize it, or correct mistakes in a related argument. Needless to say, such results have direct educational implications about how instructional materials should be organized for effective learning, and about the potential utility of teaching students general skills for organizing their own knowledge hierarchically.

A third generally significant issue arising in our work concerns the extreme importance of effective problem formulation. Indeed, how a problem is initially described, even before the planning or implementation of a solution, determines crucially how easily the problem can be solved or whether it can be solved at all. According to models prevalent in cognitive science, a person's knowledge can be imagined as decomposable into "schemas" relevant to different problem domains. Hence, it is worth studying how any such schema prescribes the way a problem should be described and specifies the particular concepts that should be used in such a description. Such questions can probably be particularly well studied in a relatively simple and well-defined domain, such as basic physics. (As a trivial example, the schema of "electric circuit problems" specifies that the appropriate concepts useful for description are "currents" and "potential drops." Deliberate redescription of any circuit problem in terms of these particular concepts does, indeed, often greatly facilitate the solution of such a problem.)

As a last example of work relevant to human cognitive engineering, I mention work motivated by developments in computers and artificial intelligence. People such as John Seely Brown and Ira Goldstein have been exploiting these developments to design "intelligent" computer-aided instructional systems that have genuine expertise about the knowledge domain to be taught, that continuously gather information about student performance in order to construct a model of the student's current knowledge, and that use this information to provide optimal tutorial interaction with the student. The design of such well-engineered instructional systems, in which the human learner is a central component, encourages systematic attention to the prescriptive aspects of human cognitive functioning. For example, it becomes useful to construct theoretical models specifying how human beings can optimally acquire and improve their knowledge by using analogies, generalization, or modifications to correct inadequate knowledge. Ira Goldstein's chapter describes in greater detail work along such lines.

I hope that the preceding examples have helped to illustrate more concretely what I mean by work in human cognitive engineering. Work along these lines might ultimately help to achieve the aim, envisaged by president Cyert, of teaching students improved problem-solving skills in a manner that is not just intuitive but that is based on good theoretical models. Furthermore, such work might also satisfy Michael Scriven's suggestion of a more prescriptive approach, although it would eschew his grossly empirical attitude in favor of a mutually beneficial interplay of theory and experiment.

OPPORTUNITIES AND DIFFICULTIES

The present time is particularly opportune for systematic work on problem solving and broader aspects of human cognitive engineering. On the one hand, both cognitive psychologists and workers in artificial intelligence have recently made progress in studying increasingly complex problems relevant to practical applications. On the other hand, some educators have recently been led to a greater concern with underlying mechanisms of problem solving. Thus the time is ripe for closing existing gaps in order to achieve a symbiotic interaction of cognitive scientists and persons interested in practical education.

Furthermore, impressive advances in electronics are rapidly increasing the power, and decreasing the costs, of computers and other information-processing technology. Hence, such technology will soon become widely available in homes, schools, and other settings. By building on recent progress in the cognitive sciences and by devoting proper attention to human cognitive engineering, one could exploit a unique opportunity to use new technology for worthy educational and human aims. Otherwise, new widespread technological capabilities may well remain unexploited or be misused.

However, work in human cognitive engineering does present some difficulties. Some of these difficulties are intrinsic and intellectual. It is not easy to explicate tacit knowledge or to formulate useful prescriptive models of human cognitive performance. Moreover, it is experimentally more difficult to test models on human subjects than on easily manipulable and reproducible computers.

Other difficulties are social and institutional. Anyone presently interested in human cognitive engineering is working in somewhat of a no-man's land between established disciplines. He or she would be regarded neither as a cognitive psychologist nor as a member of the "artificial intelligentsia"—nor as someone belonging to the traditional community of educators. Such a person may thus have difficulties finding appropriate colleagues, having access to suitable professional societies or journals, or obtaining financial support from foundations that usually tend to fund work along fashionable paradigms. Furthermore, little or no help can be expected from universities. It may well be true that universities *should* be interested in furthering work in human cognitive engineering, because it is both intellectually exciting and directly germane to improving the universities' educational functions. But, in practice, most universities today are departmentally compartmentalized bureaucratic institutions, characterized more by inertia than any significant ability to provide leadership in new domains. Thus president Cyert is unfortunately quite correct in his remark that "it is easier to move a graveyard than a faculty."

But the preceding difficulties are those likely to be encountered in any new or unfashionable field. It would be most unfortunate if such difficulties discouraged talented individuals from venturing into new domains that are intellectually exciting and socially important. Thus it is my hope that the present Conference may help to bridge the existing gaps and further systematic work on human cognitive processes, especially work designed to enhance human problem-solving capabilities and to improve educational effectiveness.

RESEARCH

5 Developing a Computational Representation for Problem-Solving Skills

Ira Goldstein[1]
Massachusetts Institute of Technology

ABSTRACT

This chapter describes the evolution of a problem-solving model over several generations of *computer coaches.* Computer coaching is a type of computer-assisted instruction in which the coaching program observes the performance of a student engaged in some intellectual game. The coach's function is to intervene occasionally in student-generated situations to discuss appropriate skills that might improve the student's play. Coaching is a natural context in which to investigate the teaching and learning processes, but it is a demanding task. The computer must be able to analyze the student's performance in terms of a model of the underlying problem-solving skills. This model must represent not only expertise for the task but also intermediate stages of problem-solving skill and typical difficulties encountered by the learner. Implementing several generations of computer coaches to meet these demands has resulted in a model that represents problem-solving skills as an *evolving set of rules* for a domain acting on an *evolving representation of the problem* and executed by a *resource-limited problem solver.* This chapter describes this evolution from its starting point as a simple rule-based approach to its current form.

Keywords: Information-processing psychology, artificial intelligence, computer-assisted instruction, cognitive science, knowledge representation, computer games.

[1]The author is now at the Xerox Palo Alto Research Center, 3333 Coyote Hill Road, Palo Alto, Calif. 94304.

For several years, we have employed an unusual methodology to study problem-solving skills[2]. Rather than observing students interacting with *human teachers,* we have observed their interactions with *computer coaches.* This has provided us with a controlled environment for studying teaching and learning. Our evaluation measure has been the adequacy of a problem-solving theory to support successful tutoring by the coaching program.

Developing a computational representation for problem-solving skills is obviously difficult. Hence, our strategy has been to develop this representation in an incremental way:

- The first step introduced a representation for expertise as a set of rules. This gave the coach a description of the goal state of the teaching process.
- The second step added a representation for the *evolution of these rules* in which different levels of skill were described explicitly.
- The third step added a representation for the *data structures* employed by the student, since his problem-solving skills clearly include strategies for structuring the problem.
- The fourth step added a representation for the *cognitive resources* of the student, since otherwise the coach could not distinguish between problems requiring the same skills but making different demands on memory and processing power.

Before recounting this evolution, it is useful to observe that our research differs significantly from traditional studies of problem solving typified by Polya (1957). Polya concentrates on enumerating useful heuristics. Our research is complementary, being less concerned with problem-solving heuristics than with arriving at a general representation for such heuristics within the overall problem-solving context. Hence, many of our rules are domain specific. But the overall architecture—a processor applying rules, manipulating data structures, and constructing new rules from old—is general. In a sense, we have focused more on the *form* than on the *content* of problem solving. However, deriving a better understanding of the architecture of problem solving is crucial if we are to embed the presentation of particular problem-solving skills within a more comprehensible framework. It is also crucial if we are to develop an improved educational technology based on computers.

---

[2]This chapter describes research done with my students and colleagues at MIT, especially Jim Stansfield, Brian Carr, Kurt van Lehn, Barbara White, David Ihrie, and Sandor Schoichet. It has also benefited from a close collaboration with John Seely Brown and his colleagues at Bolt, Beranek and Newman.

COMPUTER COACHING IS AN ADVANCED FORM
OF COMPUTER-ASSISTED INSTRUCTION

In traditional computer-assisted instruction, the computer's understanding is minimal. Generally, the material is represented as a script, and the computer's function is to direct the presentation of material based on keyword responses to preprogrammed queries. Computer coaching, however, does not allow such cookbook methods. The coach must advise players in a constantly changing context. To meet this objective, coaching systems have the structure shown in Fig. 5.1.

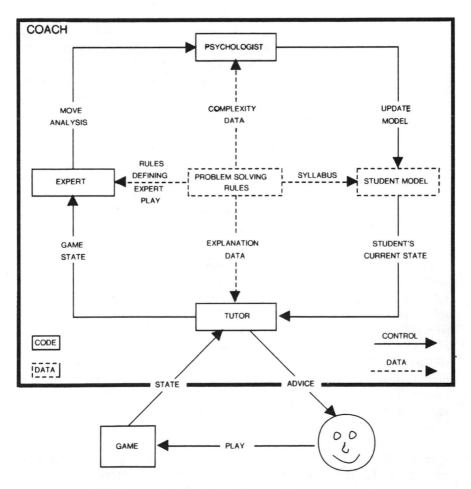

FIG. 5.1.   A simplified, block diagram of a computer coach.

- The *Expert* module generates solutions to the student's problem. Within the game context, these solutions are analyses of the pros and cons of alternative moves. To formulate these analyses, the Expert uses a procedural representation of problem-solving skills for the domain. Thus the design of the expert requires a formal and complete study of the knowledge demanded by the task.

- The *Psychologist* module must compare the Expert's analysis with the student's performance to hypothesize which skills the student understands. These hypotheses are stored in an *Overlay Model,* a term I use to emphasize that the model is defined in terms of the coach's overall understanding of the problem domain. Inferring this model is a difficult task for human teachers. Hence, if the computer coach is to succeed in its restricted world, it must take recognizance of as many sources of evidence as we can make available to it. Therefore, the design of the Psychologist focuses on developing programs to examine the student's play, ask occasional questions, request a background questionnaire, and assess the intrinsic complexity of material in the syllabus.

- The *Tutor* module is alerted by the Psychologist to situations in which the student has not employed a skill and hence made a less than optimal move. The Tutor must then decide whether to intervene and how much to say. This decision is made by employing a set of teaching heuristics. Hence, the design of the Tutor directly raises both educational questions related to the nature of explanations and linguistic questions related to the expression of these explanations in English.

Thus coaching systems are complex, requiring a representation both of the skills to be taught and of the procedures by which modeling and tutoring can be accomplished. Our coaching programs reflect this complexity both in their size (several hundred thousand words of code) and their development time (typically several man years). To date, coaching experiments have been conducted for a limited but interesting range of domains including geography (Carbonell, 1970), electronic troubleshooting (Brown, Burton, & Bell, 1975), nuclear magnetic resonance spectra analysis (Sleeman, 1975), medical diagnosis (Clancey, 1979), programming (Miller, 1979) and mathematical games (Burton & Brown, 1979; Goldstein & Carr, 1977).

In this chapter, however, I shall eschew the broad view by applying a microscope to the central box of Fig. 5.1. Developing a satisfactory representation for problem-solving skills is clearly essential to the design of coaches, as the centrality of the box in the diagram indicates.

THE WUMPUS GAME HAS SERVED AS
OUR EXPERIMENTAL TESTBED

In 1975, we began an examination of procedural models for problem solving in a game environment. We chose a game environment based on Burton and Brown's (1979) experience with a coach for the Plato project's arithmetic game *How the West was Won.*[3] They found games to be a motivating but nevertheless constrained environment that was well suited to the coaching paradigm.

Following Burton and Brown's lead, we designed a coach for *Wumpus,* a computer game invented by Gregory Yob (1975). The game is a modern day *Theseus and the Minotaur,* in which the player's goal is to slay the Wumpus. The game's virtue is that an interesting variety of logical and probabilistic reasoning skills are required to play skillfully. To define the game, I have reproduced the introduction printed by the coach.

You are a world-renowned hunter descending down into the caves of darkness, lair of the infamous man-eating Wumpus. To the win the game, you must kill the Wumpus by shooting one of your five arrows into his lair from a neighboring cave. If you go into the cave of the Wumpus he will eat you. Within the warren there are two other kinds of dangers, bats and pits. The pits are bottomless and fatal if you fall into one of them. If you visit the home cave of bats they will pick you up and carry you to another cave which might contain the Wumpus or a pit (either of which is fatal).

You can gain information about the warren through exploration. If bats are in one of the neighboring caves you will hear their high-pitched squeaking. Likewise, if you are next to a cave with a pit you will feel draft. If you are near the Wumpus, you will smell his horrible stench.

Before you shoot an arrow, you should consider the fact that if the Wumpus is not in the cave, the arrow will start ricocheting and may kill you (and it is an agonizing death). If it does start ricocheting, there is roughly a one third chance that it will kill you. If you run out of arrows without slaying the Wumpus, you are doomed to wander forever until you die.

Your only companion in this endeavor is the wise old sage, Wusor. If you make a hasty move, Wusor may stop you and give you advice, but the final decision rests with you.

---

[3]*West* is a simple board game in which the player moves by forming an arithmetic expression from three spinners. The game is race, and hence the player's usual goal is to form the largest expression, with the typical alternatives of bumping your opponent or landing on special squares. The student gains experience with arithmetic by searching for the optimal expression. The coach tracks the student's choice of move and offers advice about arithmetic skills not being employed by the student in situations where their use would be of value.

Following this introduction, a typical game might proceed as follows. The student is Mary, a 12-year-old player.

> Hi Mary. There are 15 caves, 2 bats, 2 pits, and 1 Wumpus. You are at cave 15 with neighbors 4, 14, and 0. Brrr! There is a draft. You are near a pit. What now?
>
> > 4
>
> You are at cave 4 with neighbors 15, 14, and 2. Brrr! There is a draft. Squeak! A bat is near.

As Fig. 5.2 illustrates, many players draw maps and/or tables to keep track

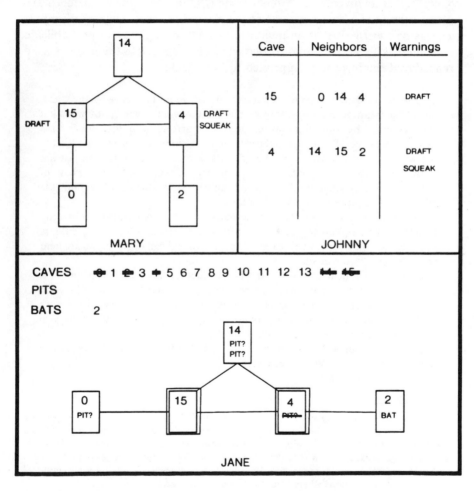

FIG. 5.2.   Player's representations of the game.

of their exploration of the warren. Figure 5.2 shows the map drawn by Mary for this purpose as well as alternative representations employed by other students.

Wumpus is colorful and challenging, thereby capturing the interest of a wide range of players. Adults typically invest several hours to master the game, children several days or weeks. Locating multiple dangers in a randomly connected warren requires skills of logical deduction, probabilistic inference, problem representation, and overall strategy selection. For example, consider Mary's situation:

1. From a *logical* standpoint, Mary should infer that cave 2 contains a bat since (a) the *squeak* in Cave 4 implies that a bat is in either Cave 2 or 14; but (b) the absence of a squeak in Cave 15 rules out Cave 14 as a possibility. As Mary's game progresses, opportunities will be commonplace for arguments by elimination, by cases, or by contradiction.

2. From a *probabilistic* standpoint, Mary should infer that Cave 14 is more dangerous with respect to pits than Cave 0 or 2 on the basis of the multiple warnings. The multiple warnings for a pit do not determine the location of the danger. (If there were only one pit, this would be not be true.) But multiple warnings do imply that Cave 14 should be treated as more likely to contain the pit. An expert player typically makes approximate numerical judgments of the probabilities when logical inferences are insufficient to locate safe caves.

3. From a *problem-representation* standpoint, Mary's map is a useful artifact for representing the problem. Many students initially choose tables, which make deductions about connectivity difficult. There are, however, other representational devices such as lists or tables that prove useful. The most challenging aspect of the game for many players is to derive an adequate representational scheme.

4. From a *strategic* standpoint, Mary must recognize that her goal is to avoid the more dangerous caves while still gaining information about the warren. Strategic considerations grow more complex as the number of arrows are exhausted or as the time to complete the game grows short.

This analysis only sketches the requisite knowledge, but it demonstrates that skilled play does pose an intellectual challenge. Indeed, the game is sufficiently complex to exhibit a *plateau phenomenon* in which players occasionally stagnate at particular levels of skill. Tutoring is then required to facilitate further learning. Hence, the game is not an artificial environment in which to study problem solving.

OUR FIRST STEP WAS TO
REPRESENT PROBLEM-SOLVING SKILLS
AS A SET OF RULES

In 1976, we implemented a coach in which the mathematical and probabilistic skills needed to play Wumpus were represented by approximately 25 rules (Goldstein & Carr, 1977). The rules fell into two categories: those that deduced evidence about the warren, and those that made strategic decisions on the basis of that evidence:

Typical Evidence Rules.   These rules construct sets of caves that represent hypotheses about the locations of different dangers. The context for all of these rules is that the player has just entered a cave in the warren and been told its neighbors and its warnings.

> *ER1:*   Add the unvisited neighbors to the set of *fringe* caves. The *fringe* set records those caves that have not yet been visited but can be reached from the player's current location in the warren.
>
> *ER2P:*   If there is not a pit warning, then add the neighbors to *PIT−*. *PIT−* is the set of caves that do *not* risk pits.
>
> *ER3P:*   If there is a pit warning, then add the neighbors to *PIT+* . *PIT+* is the set of caves that risk pits.
>
> *ER5P:*   If there is a pit warning and one of the neighbors is already in *PIT+* , then add that neighbor to *PIT2*. *PIT2* is the set of caves for which the player has multiple evidence of a pit.
>
> *ER6P:*   If there is a pit warning and all but one of the neighbors are known to be safe, then add that neighbor to *PIT=*. *PIT=* is the set of caves that definitely contain a pit.

Similar rules are defined for the other dangers. The convention is employed that special case rules for particular dangers are given names ending with the suffixes *B, P,* or *W.*

Typical Strategy Rules.   These rules are concerned with choosing the move based on the available evidence.

> *SR0:*   Shoot an arrow if the Wumpus' lair is found; that is, shoot if a cave is added to *WUM=*.
>
> *SR1:*   Explore safe caves, that is, explore any caves in the intersection of *PIT−*, *BAT−,* and *WUM−*.
>
> *SR2:*   Explore caves implicated by single warnings before caves implicated by multiple warnings; that is, if possible, prefer caves that are not in *danger2* sets.
>
> *SR3:*   Explore caves that only risk bats; that is, prefer elements of *BAT+*.
>
> *SR4:*   If no other strategy rule applies, explore any available fringe cave (i.e., any member of *fringe).*

Similar strategy rules express preferences for other combinations of risk as recorded in the various evidence sets.

These rules were applied in a fixed order, with the strategy rules being more sensitive to the ordering chosen than the evidence rules.

These rules are problem-specific. Hence, the question arises whether or not the coach conveys any general problem-solving knowledge. My reply is that these rules implicitly embody important general skills such as: (1) argument by elimination; (2) the use of sets to represent hypotheses; and (3) the sequential organization of a set of heuristics. It is true that the coach does not understand them in this fashion: Its orientation is problem-specific. However, a reasonable hypothesis is that general problem-solving skills can be profitably taught through problem-solving specific situations. This is not a radical position, since it accords with the traditional philosophy of *learning by doing*. Eventually, we will conduct experiments to learn if the implicit skills of Wumpus do transfer to other situations. But our current focus is on the prerequisite goal of developing an adequate representational formalism to incorporate the required problem-solving knowledge into a coach.

Within the computer, these rules are represented as a set of attribute value pairs. The description for ER3P is shown in Table 5.1. The rules are represented in this form, rather than as lines of code in a large program, to allow the coach to diagnose situations in which the student has pieces of procedural knowledge but applies them in the wrong order.

Based on these rules, the coach was able to offer the following kind of advice. Mary has just chosen to move to Cave 14 in the situation illustrated in Fig. 5.2:

> *Explanation E1:* Mary, it isn't necessary to take such risks with pits. Multiple evidence is more dangerous than single evidence for pits. Here there is multiple evidence for a pit in 14 and single evidence for a pit in 0. Perhaps we should explore Cave 0 instead. Do you want to take back your move?

This explanation was generated by a set of templates applied to a *proof* generated by the Expert module that move 0 is better than move 14. The term *proof* is legitimate when the rules are viewed as theorems of the domain. For

TABLE 5.1
Description of Rule *ER3P*

Attribute	Value
Type	Evidence rule
English	If a cave has a draft, then the neighbors possibly risk pits.
Condition	Is "draft" a warning of the current cave?
Action	Add the neighbors of the current cave to PIT+.

example, the Expert produces the following (simplified) analysis. The analysis is expressed in English rather than the equivalent internal computer representation:

There is no squeak in Cave 15.	;Given
Therefore, Cave 0 is a member of bat–.	;By evidence rule *ER2B*.
There is a draft in Cave 15.	;Given
Therefore, Cave 0 is a member of pit+.	;By evidence rule *ER3P*.
There is a draft in Cave 15 and Cave 4.	;Given
Therefore, Cave 14 is a member of pit2.	;By evidence rule *ER5P*.
Conclusion, 0 is superior to 14.	;By strategy rule *SR2*.

Thus our first Coach was essentially a *mathematician* in the sense that it viewed the tutoring process from the theorem-proving standpoint. Its goal was to inform the student of the bugs in his *proof* of the current situation. Our experience with this coach was that students generally enjoyed its advice. And, upon occasion, it successfully prodded students off plateaus by making them aware of poor moves. However, viewing students as mathematicians who need only be told the appropriate theorems is clearly insufficient as a model of the learning process. The next section discusses how the addition of historical perspective on the development of these theorems significantly improves the coach's explanatory power.

OUR SECOND STEP WAS TO REPRESENT PROBLEM-SOLVING SKILLS AS AN *EVOLVING* SET OF RULES

To appreciate why a historical perspective of problem-solving skills must supplement the coach's basic mathematical understanding, it is useful to reexamine the advice offered Mary in the previous section. Recall that she has made a poor move to Cave 14. The mathematical explanation provided is that she has failed to apply the *double evidence* theorem. The central assertion was:

Explanation E1: Mary, it isn't necessary to take such large risks with pits. Multiple evidence is more dangerous than single evidence for pits....

This advice might be sufficient. Indeed, in our experience, it is just right for some students. But the explanation does not take advantage of Mary's history. For example, if she has recently encountered a similar situation for another kind of danger, then an explanation that emphasized the analogy would be appropriate.

Explanation E2: Mary, it isn't necessary to take such large risks with pits. We have seen that multiple evidence is more dangerous than single evidence *for bats....*

Or, alternatively, an explanation that emphasized the relevant generalization would be appropriate.

Explanation E3: Mary, it isn't necessary to take such large risks with pits. Multiple evidence is more dangerous than single evidence *for all dangers....*

Finally, the explanation might emphasize the relationship of the new strategy to an earlier, simplified view of the game.

Explanation E4: Mary, it isn't necessary to take such large risks with pits. *In the past, we have distinguished between safe and dangerous evidence.* Now we should distinguish between single and multiple evidence for a danger.

I am not saying that any one explanation is the *correct* one. However, I am saying that a model of learning and teaching must make provision for these alternatives. A teacher can then move among them as the student's history and responses suggest.

The first *mathematician* coach did not have this flexibility. Its point of view was essentially that the student was an *"empty bucket"* in which knowledge was to be poured until skilled performance was achieved. At any moment in time, the coach viewed the student's skills as a subset of those of the expert. It ignored the fact that acquisition of skills is a more complex process involving the use of analogies, generalizations, and corrections to build new rules from previously acquired ones. This ignorance was reflected in its inability to structure an explanation in these terms. Clearly what was needed was an extended representation for describing the evolution of procedural knowledge from one level of skill to another.

We provided this extended representation by employing a network formalism in which rules were represented as nodes and their evolutionary relationships as labeled links between these nodes. These labels designated various relationships by which one rule might be built from another, including generalization, specialization, analogy, and refinement. Figure 5.3 is a region of the Wumpus rule network that exhibits these relationships. Examine Rule *ER1* of Fig. 5.3. It is a general statement that *"If a warning occurs, then the neighbors for the current cave should be added to the set D+ representing possibly dangerous caves."* *ER3* is a generalization of particular rules for bats, pits, and Wumpi. This is represented in the network by *specialization* links to *ER3B, ER3P,* and *ER3W.* (There are inverse *generalization* links from *ER3B, ER3P,* and *ER3W* to *ER3* that are not

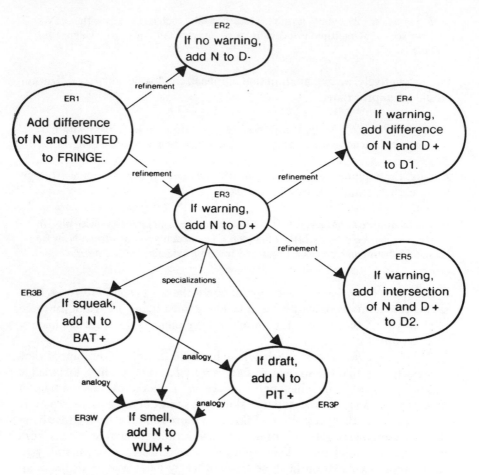

FIG. 5.3.   A region of the Wumpus skill network concerned with evidence rules.

shown.) Each of the specializations is connected to its brothers by *analogy* links. The analogy relationship is defined formally by the existence of a mapping from the variables of one special case rule to another. Finally, *ER3* is connected by *refinement* links to *ER4* and *ER5*. A refinement is defined by breaking a rule's *condition* or *action* into separate cases. Thus *ER4* and *ER5* are produced by breaking the action of *ER3* into two cases: one for single evidence and one for double evidence. *ER3* was in turn refined from *ER1* by breaking the condition of that rule into two cases: one for warnings and one for no warnings.

There is another vantage point from which to view the network. This is from the local perspective of an individual rule rather than from the global

TABLE 5.2
Extended Description of Rule *ER3P*

Comment: This is the basic rule description	
Attribute	*Value*
Type	Evidence rule
English	If a cave has a draft, then the neighbors possibly risk pits.
Condition	Is "draft" a warning of the current cave?
Action	Add the neighbors of the current cave to PIT+.
Comment: These relations define the skill network.	
Analogous-to	*ER3B ER3W*
Specialization-of	*ER3*

perspective of the overall network. Recall that our first representation viewed rules in isolation: Their description contained only properties for their condition and action. From a local perspective, the rule network is a *derived* structure that arises from augmenting individual rule descriptions with special connections to related rules. The rule description thus characterizes rules as members of a society with both internal and external relationships. In fact, the actual computer representation takes this form. Each rule is supplied with an augmented description, of which Table 5.2 is typical. The network itself is derived from the connections between rules specified in the analogy, specialization, and refinement attributes.

The coach cannot perform the learning processes specified by these attributes: The programmer supplied these interrelationships. However, given the availability of this network representation of the skills to be taught the new coach now being completed will be capable of a more diverse set of explanations. The variations *E2, E3,* and *E4* will be generated by using English templates to be triggered by the existence of evolutionary links between the specific rule that "double evidence for pits is more dangerous than single evidence" and other rules in the skill network. The region of the skill network containing this rule is shown in Fig. 5.4, embedded within an overlay model describing the student's knowledge state. The relationship of the network to the student model is the subject of the next section.

Extending the Coach's Representation of Problem-Solving Skills Improves Its Student Modeling Capabilities

The coach models the student by identifying which pieces of its problem-solving knowledge are apparently employed by the student. I have termed this kind of model an Overlay model to emphasize its dependence on the coach's

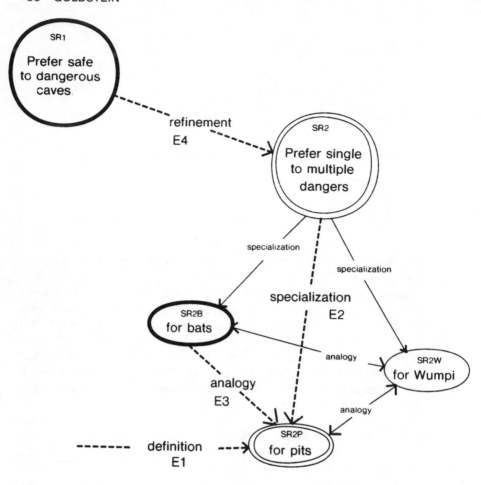

FIG. 5.4.   An overlay model for a region of the skill network.

understanding of the task. With the extension of this understanding from a list of rules to a network, modeling includes both identifying the skill nodes employed by the student and the evolutionary links followed in the acquisition process. Figure 5.4 is a graphic representation of an overlay model maintained by the coach. The coach keeps track of which rules it believes the student already possesses on the basis of his or her behavior as well as the explanations it has offered to facilitate this learning process.

The computer represents an Overlay model as additional information within each rule description. Thus the description for *SR2P* would include the properties listed in Table 5.3.

TABLE 5.3
Description of Rule *SR2P*

Attribute	Value	
Comment: This is the basic rule description. It is this strategy rule that objects to Mary's choice of Cave 14 as her move.		
Type	Strategy-rule	
English	If there are caves that only possibly risk pits, move there.	
Condition	Is *PIT1* a non-empty set?	
Action	Set moves, the set from which the next move will be chosen, to *PIT1*.	
Comment: Overlay model information for this rule.		
Explanations	E1	:*E1* is the explanation just given to Mary regarding the inadvisability of moving to Cave 14.
Used	0	;The coach believes that Mary has never used this rule.
Appropriate	1	;The coach believes that the rule has been appropriate once. In this case, this is in choosing not to move to Cave 14.
Frequency	0	;"Frequency" is the ratio of "used" to "appropriate" and represents an estimate of how frequently Mary employs this skill. For *SR2P*, the coach believes that Mary has never employed this rule.
Knows	No	;"Knows" records the coach's hypothesis for whether or not Mary knows this rule. It is "no" if the "Frequency" is less than .5.

A Student Simulator Was Implemented To Explore the Behavior of Different Skill Models

The Student Simulator is an environment for executing the rules specified in an Overlay model. Its function is to allow a teacher to explore the behavioral implications of different hypotheses about a student's skills. Its value rises in those situations in which the teacher is unable to predict a priori the divergent behavior implied by different student models for complex problem-solving situations.[4]

---

[4]Brown and Burton (1978, pp. 170–171) have demonstrated another utility of a student simulator, and this is as an environment in which student teachers can gain experience in building models of their pupils. They exposed student teachers to a simulator for elementary arithmetic skills. Their results showed that exposure to their simulator significantly improved the student teacher's ability to diagnose procedural bugs in a student's behavior.

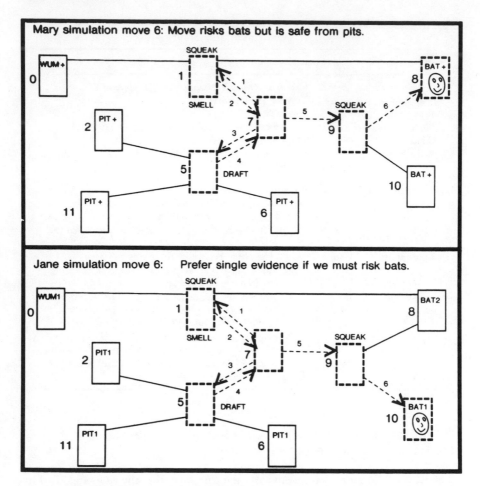

FIG. 5.5.   Divergent behavior of two simulated students. (Dashed arrows signify the path of the simulated student.)

Figure 5.5 illustrates the simulator by showing a trace of two simulated students on the same game. The simulation in the upper half of the figure employs the rules specified by Mary's overlay model. This rule set does not take account of double evidence, as was reflected in Mary's earlier choice of Cave 14. (See Fig. 5.2.) Hence, when faced with the choice of Cave 8 or Cave 10, it chooses Cave 8, the riskier of the two. The simulator prints the explanatory message for the choice of move 6 by fetching a description of the strategy rule that governed the decision. The second simulation is constructed from the overlay model for Jane, a more advanced player who does distinguish between single and multiple evidence as reflected in her use of *BAT1* and *BAT2* markers. (See Fig. 5.2 for Jane's representation of the warren.) Here the Jane simulacrum correctly chooses Cave 10 as the better move. Hence, the simulator can serve a teacher who is interested in understanding the different behavior that two skill models might produce.

OUR THIRD STEP WAS TO
REPRESENT THE EXTERNAL DATA STRUCTURES
EMPLOYED BY THE STUDENT

Supplying a historical perspective improves the range of explanations that the coach can deliver, but it is not sufficient as a *teachable* model of the problem-solving process. Absent is a representation of the objects on which problem-solving rules operate. The coach, as yet, has no understanding of the problems involved in formulating a representation of the problem. Being both mathematician and historian is insufficient: The coach must also be an *epistemologist*. A more careful scrutiny of the knowledge demanded by the problem-solving process is in order.

Out attention was focused on the need to consider the student's representation of the state of the game, its history, and his or her hypotheses about the task by the following kind of situation. Students would frequently be able to explain a skill in isolation yet not apply it when appropriate. This point was illustrated by experiments we conducted in which two populations of students were exposed to Wumpus with different aids to represent the game. Some were provided with only pencil and paper—others with a display version of the game on which a map was automatically drawn. The latter group played a much superior game of Wumpus, yet statistically both groups possessed the same skills.

Hence, it was necessary to extend our representation of problem solving to include a representation of the evolving data representations employed by the student. To guide this extension, we observed the various representations employed by students, as illustrated in Fig. 5.2. We observed that some students built data representations that reflected their ignorance of the importance of certain information: For example, Mary did not realize that distinguishing single from multiple warnings for a danger was useful. Other students assumed too much: A common bug of younger players was assuming that caves were connected if they were drawn close to one another on the map. Still a third group of students created representations that proved adequate while the game was simple but failed when its demands grew complex. Johnny's table will make inferences about the connectivity of the warren complex as the game progresses. On the other hand, a fourth class of students employed redundant representations to facilitate different inferences. For example, Jane drew both a map and a list of visited caves. She used the former to reason about connectivity and the latter to infer the location of dangers by a process of elimination.

A Display-Based Wumpus Game Was Implemented
To Explore the Role of Data Representation

To explore the role of data and hypothesis representations in problem solving, we have implemented a display-based Wumpus in which the student can manipulate different data structures. The student is not allowed pencil and paper; hence, his or her entire external representation is in a form that the computer coach can observe. Display Wumpus allows the student or the coach to select various data representations for the connectivity of the warren and for hypotheses formulated by the student regarding dangers from among those shown in Fig. 5.6. Here are some of the choices that Display Wumpus permits:

1. The warren can be described via the usual teletype description that prints the current caves, its neighbors, and its warnings, or via a map.

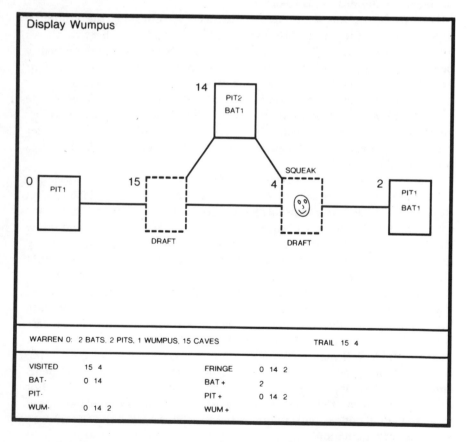

FIG. 5.6.   The map and list representations provided by Display Wumpus.

2. Caves that the player has visited can be represented either by dashing their outline or in the list labeled *visited*.
3. The player's current location can be represented either by the cave with the face or by the last entry to the *trail* list.
4. A hypothesis that a cave risks a particular danger can be grouped either under the heading of the cave (on the map) or under the heading of the danger (in the tabular evidence area).

These representations are only a subset of those that a student might design on his or her own. We have restricted the student's freedom in return for increasing the coach's insight into the problem solving. However, Display Wumpus is only an experimental tool. To make it into a useful educational environment, Display Wumpus could be provided with a *tablet* device so that students can design their own representations while still allowing the coach to observe their behavior.

Formally, Display Wumpus is based on the following point of view. For each type of evidence (that is, input and output variable of a rule), there is a set of possible external representations. For Wumpus, these representations include tables, maps, and the null representation—that is, no external representation at all. This selection of possible external representations is based on our experiments with children. We typically found an evolution of representation from the null representation, to tables like Johnny's, to maps like Mary's, to combined representations like Jane's. We have also seen "representation traps" in which the player persists with a given representation, say Johnny's tabular representation of the maze, and consequently finds it extremely difficult to progress to the acquisition of more complex reasoning strategies.

We Are Now in the Process of Implementing a Coach for Display Wumpus

The current Display Wumpus has served as an experimental medium for several months in which we have observed the untutored play of many students. We are now designing a coach to take advantage of the larger window for observing the student's play that it provides. The new coach will maintain an overlay model of the student's use of the data representations supplied by Display Wumpus. For example, consider again Mary's map of Fig. 5.2. If this map is drawn with Display Wumpus, then the coach would construct the description in Table 5.4 to supplement its overlay model of her problem-solving skills.

With this description, the coach will be capable of explaining a certain representation if it believes that the student knows the appropriate rules but is not representing the data in a way that would make their application evident. For example, suppose that Johnny selected Cave 14 as his next move. Recall

TABLE 5.4
Description of Mary's Problem Representation

Attribute	Value	
Warning-representation	Map	;Mary records the draft on the map
Neighbor-representation	Map	;and the neighbors,
Danger-representation	None	;but not the caves that risk pits,
Visited-representation	None	;nor the visited caves.

that earlier, when Mary selected this move, the coach discussed with her the increased danger implied by double evidence. But Johnny's problem may simply be that he does not realize that Cave 0 is implicated both by the warning in Cave 15 and the warning in Cave 4. His tabular representation requires that he infer that 14 is connected to both by examining two rows of the table. It is not as easy an inference as it is for Mary with her graphic representation of the warren. In this situation, we envision the following dialog:

> *Explanation E5:*   Johnny, do you realize that Cave 14 is risky both because of the warning in Cave 15 and the warning in Cave 4? Using tables makes this difficult to see. Perhaps you would like to employ a map?

The coach would then instruct Display Wumpus to provide a map similar to the one shown in Fig 5.6 but simplified by removing the danger symbols (*PIT1, PIT2*, etc.). These symbols along with the list representation would not be offered, because Johnny's level of play does not yet warrant proposing this additional machinery. Johnny could then choose to employ the map by using the appropriate drawing commands of Display Wumpus. Thus the coach does not engage in a discussion of the probabilities implied by double evidence but addresses the prerequisite task of helping Johnny with his representation.

OUR FOURTH STEP WAS TO
REPRESENT THE RESOURCE LIMITATIONS
OF THE PROBLEM SOLVER

In the previous section we provided the coach with knowledge regarding the various data structures a student might employ to represent the problem. This knowledge is necessary but not sufficient to guide the coach in its generation of explanations like *E5*; such knowledge does not determine *when* the corresponding advice is appropriate. For example, in the above situation, it may be premature to suggest a map to Johnny. The game may still be too simple to stress the table representation. Tutoring leverage will not exist until Johnny perceives the inadequacies of his current representation scheme relative to the complexity of the problem. Thus whether or not advice about a change in representation is appropriate depends on an estimate of the cognitive load that the problem imposes on the student. Hence, an epistemologist's insight into the breadth of knowledge required by the task must be supplemented by a psychologist's insight into the relative complexity of the material.

An Elementary Method for Estimating the Complexity of the Game Was Implemented

The coach estimates the complexity of the game in terms of the number of dangers, the number of caves, the propagation distance of warnings, and the mobility of the dangers. Increasing any of these parameters is assumed to increase the complexity of the task. This is borne out by our informal experiments with students and by the intrinsic computational work that the problem solver is required to perform.

The coach currently employs its student model to guide its selection of the complexity of the Wumpus task presented to the student. The fact that Mary was presented with a game of 15 caves, 2 bats, 2 pits, and 1 stationary Wumpus was not accidental. Had she been a novice, she would have been exposed to only 1 bat, 1 pit, and a warren of 10 caves. When she becomes an expert, the Wumpus is allowed to move when attacked, and the number of bats and pits is increased to three.

A Theory-Based Estimate of Cognitive Load Is Needed

The elementary method for estimating the complexity of the game was added to the coach when it became clear that the advanced game was too complex for beginners. But this method was not based on a deep theory of cognition. Our current research addresses this issue by constructing a more formal model of the *problem solver*. Our plan is to include an explicit representation of the resources required by the problem-solving interpreter to apply a given set of skills. This would include such process-oriented parameters as: depth and breadth of the search space, the complexity of the data structures being maintained in terms of their size, the complexity of the patterns of individual rules in terms of the number of variables they access and the number of conjuncts or disjuncts in their pattern, and the number of rules matching particular patterns. It would also include a representation for memory load as reflected by the number and size of the data structures that must be maintained. The extension then is to represent various limits on these resources.

There is no a priori reason why the load points of the expert module's problem-solving program should correspond to the load points encountered by a human problem solver. Perhaps they solve problems in very different ways. This is theoretically possible. However, remember that the problem-solving skills have been formulated in a very anthropomorphic fashion. They have been carefully broken into small pieces, comprehensible to the learner. This does not guarantee a correspondence in workload, but it suggests one. Hence, our starting point for a psychological model of the student's resource limitations will be the load points of our expert program. There is a second rationale for this starting point. Recall that our orientation is teacher-centered. Hence, these load points are those suggested to a teacher beginning his or her course from a particular perspective on the syllabus. This does not obviate the need to investigate the psychological reality of this resource model: It only provides a starting point. Hence, a future goal will be to correlate this theoretically motivated formulation with the psychological literature on cognitive load. (See Norman & Bobrow, 1975, for a discussion of data-limited and resource-limited processes from a psychological perspective.)

As usual, extending the underlying problem-solving representation allows the overlay model of the student to be more accurate. The representation for this augmented model, however, goes beyond the individual rules. An explicit model of the problem solver is required. Again we propose to employ an attribute value description. The attributes are the load dimensions: The values are the thresholds at which the student is expected to falter (see Table 5.5). These thresholds are estimates based on experience with various students. The coach would have a table of such estimates for students of various age and skill backgrounds.

An interesting consequence of representing cognitive load factors is that we have a rationale for the apparently redundant data structures provided by Display Wumpus. Examine Fig. 5.6 again, and observe that the caves that risk bats are represented explicitly as a list under the label *BAT+* as well as by means of *BAT+* symbols in the appropriate caves. Logically, these representations are equivalent. But cognitively, the list representation makes it cheap to compute how many caves are among the candidates for the bat's

TABLE 5.5
Description of Mary's Problem-Solving Capacity

Representation	Estimated Confusion Threshold
Null	Set exceeds 3 elements.
List	Set exceeds 5 elements.
Map	Set exceeds 15 elements.

nest, whereas the map representation makes this expensive. The first requires a single data fetch on the *BAT+* list, whereas the second requires a data fetch on every cave to see if it contains the *BAT+* symbol. On the other hand, the map-oriented representation makes it cheap to decide if a particular cave risks bats. Thus there is a rationale for both. This is supported by our experience that expert players maintain both kinds of data structures.

Extensions to the underlying problem-solving representation also improve the utility of the Student Simulator. The performance of a particular rule model and associated data representation can be examined under different load thresholds. We plan to allow the user to set such thresholds as the maximum number of hypotheses that can be remembered implicitly with no error or the maximum number of predicates in a rule condition that can be executed with no error.

THERE ARE MORE STEPS TO BE TAKEN IN CONSTRUCTING AN ADEQUATE PROBLEM-SOLVING MODEL

This chapter has recounted the development of our problem-solving model from an unorganized set of rules to a network representation of an evolving set of rules acting on an evolving data representation and executed by a resource-limited problem solver. The forcing function has been the design of an adequate coaching system. Our response has been to provide the coach with multiple perspectives on its subject matter by incorporating the viewpoints of a *mathematician*, a *historian*, an *epistemologist*, and a *psychologist*. The result is a teaching artifact that exhibits a deeper understanding of its subject matter as exhibited by the range of explanations it can generate.

The four steps we have described, however, do not exhaust the knowledge that a problem-solving theory must represent. In this section, I enumerate several extensions, with proposals for: (1) how to incorporate them into our problem-solving model; and (2) how to extend the Wumpus game environment to improve its utility as an experimental base for examining these issues. These extensions are intended to incorporate within the coach the additional perspectives of the *manager,* and *learner,* the *scholar,* and the *bookkeeper.*

The Manager.   Our discussion of problem solving ignored the *organizational skills* needed to manage large numbers of individual skills. This management includes such functions as selecting appropriate skill sets to apply to the current problem, organizing their order of application, and removing inappropriate skill sets. In the artificial-intelligence literature, this class of problem-solving knowledge has been explored by Davis (1976) in the context of improving the problem-solving behavior of the MYCIN medical diagnosis program. Davis supplies metarules to represent this class of knowledge. The Wumpus rule network should be extended to incorporate this knowledge explicitly, providing, for example, an explicit representation of metarules for governing the order of application of individual strategies. By supplying these metarules, the coach could maintain an improved overlay model by measuring the use and appropriateness of various metastrategies in the student's play.

The Learner. Our discussion of problem solving also skirted the representation of *learning skills*. A preliminary step was taken by specifying potential evolutionary relationships between rules in the skill network, but it did not characterize the learning processes involved. Again we plan to draw from the artificial-intelligence literature. Moore and Newell (1973) describe the formal structure of analogies in terms of mappings between the attributes of the objects being compared. Hence, a natural extension of our rule network is to replace the labels on analogy links with descriptions of the mappings between the attributes of the connected rules. Such descriptions would record, for example, that bats and pits are analogous with respect to the distance their warnings propagate but not analogous with respect to the degree of danger that they imply. Doing so would allow the tutor module to be more explicit in its advice about potential analogies.

The Scholar. Another extension is required to represent *declarative knowledge*. We have taken a procedural viewpoint throughout this chapter. Adding organizational and learning skills continues in this vein. But clearly not all of an individual's problem-solving knowledge is rule-like. Such an emphasis fails to take account of the factual knowledge that an individual uses to justify the application of particular rules or to deduce those rules in the first place. The artificial-intelligence literature has explored the interplay between declarative knowledge (often expressed in the predicate calculus) and procedural knowledge. For example, Green (1969) explored the derivation of programs from proofs. This class of knowledge must ultimately be included if the coach is to understand how to offer advice that emphasizes the governing principle rather than the specific rules. As a first step, we plan to include *fact nodes* in the syllabus network to represent the logical axioms of Wumpus. For example, the axiom of Wumpus that "A cave either contains a danger or is safe, but not both" would be represented explicitly. This fact justifies several rules but is not itself explicitly procedural. The fact node would be linked to the rules it justifies. By adding these fact nodes, we will improve both the overlay modeling capability of the coach and the range of advice that can be offered.

The Bookkeeper. In our emphasis on rules, we have also largely ignored the *episodic structure of memory*. The coach is based on the presumption that tutoring by example is fundamental to learning. But the coach has no representation for the interrelationships between particular tutorial episodes and the rules they explain. Consistent with the four steps taken in this chapter, our plan is to broaden the attribute description of individual rules by providing links to nodes describing tutorial interactions with the student. This should have a visible return by giving the coach the ability to estimate whether or not a particular rule will be remembered. The coach could base this hypothesis on the number of explanations, their frequency, and their recency, all of which would be recorded in the extended rule description.

To increase our leverage to explore these extensions, we intend to generalize the Wumpus game by multiplying its cast of characters. We plan to extend its fairy tale motif by adding such characters as dwarves, dragons, princes, and princesses. Each character will have its own kind of behavior and generate its own kind of evidence. We expect that these extensions will bring into clearer focus the *organizational skills* for managing larger sets of problem-solving heuristics; the *learning skills* for taking advantage of the larger number of possible analogies, generalizations, and refinements that the extended world suggests; and the *memory skills* for properly organizing a more diverse set of experiences. However, these extensions still preserve the closed and tractable properties of the game environment that make it a desirable experimental domain.

A COMPUTATIONAL THEORY OF PROBLEM SOLVING HAS MANY EDUCATIONAL APPLICATIONS

Predicting drastic reductions in the cost of computers is now commonplace. Less clearly foreseen is their potential to perform as *problem-solving tools*. Of course, a calculator is such a tool. But I have in mind a more extensive role for these machines in which they truly know something about the task and contribute accordingly. In this chapter, we consider only the coaching role. However, here are three related roles that, like the coach, are based upon a computational representation for problem-solving skills:

1. Computers could serve as *personal assistants* in which the computer assumes some part of the problem-solving task, thereby freeing the student to solve more complex problems. Display Wumpus is a simple example of such an assistant. It demonstrated the fashion in which appropriate design can free students to reason about the logical

complexity of the game without being confused by its geometric structure.

2. Computers could provide *cognitive programming environments* in which students implement their own problem-solving programs. In this fashion, students can gain a more intimate understanding of the subject matter in an active and exciting fashion. To explore this role, we are developing a Programmable Wumpus in which the student does not play but, rather, specifies the rules to be employed by a computer player who represents him on the playing field. Thus the student acquires experience with problem solving by acting as the teacher rather than the student.

3. Computers could provide *cognitive simulation environments* in which the consequences of various learning and teaching strategies are explored. Our Student Simulator is a forerunner of this application. Potentially such simulations could serve the same role in education as wind tunnels do in aeronautics—namely, a low-cost, low-risk environment for examining the behavior of scale models of students.

The potential impact of computers as problem-solving tools is interesting to project, but clearly this projection must not blind us to the many difficult problems that must first be solved. These problems do not lie in building powerful hardware but, rather, in developing an adequate understanding of the problem-solving process. This chapter has described one methodology for acquiring this understanding—the development of computer coaches. Future research will undoubtedly include the development of consultants, assistants, and simulators as additional instruments for stressing and testing our theories of cognitive skills.

ACKNOWLEDGMENTS

This research was supported, in part, by NSF grant SED77-19279 and, in part, by the MIT Division for Study and Research in Education.

REFERENCES

Brown, J. S., & Burton, R. Diagnostic models for procedural bugs in basic mathematical skills. *Cognitive Science,* 1978, *2,* 155–192.

Brown, J. S., Burton, R., & Bell, A. SOPHIE: A step toward creating a reactive learning environment. *International Journal of Man–Machine Studies,* 1975, *7,* 675–696.

Burton, R., & Brown, J. S. An investigation of computer coaching for informal learning activities. *International Journal of Man–Machine Studies,* 1979, *11,* 5–24.

Carbonell, J. AI in CAI: An artificial-intelligence approach to computer-assisted instruction. *IEEE Transactions on Man-Machine Systems,* December 1970, *MMS-11* (4).

Clancey, W. B. Tutoring rules for guiding a case method dialogue. *International Journal of Man-Machine Studies,* 1979, *11,* 25–49.

Davis, R. Applications of meta level knowledge to the construction, maintenance and use of large knowledge bases (Stanford AI Memo 283). Stanford, Calif.: University of Stanford, July 1976.

Goldstein, I., & Carr, B. The computer as coach: An athletic paradigm for intellectual education. *Proceedings of 1977 Annual Conference, Association for Computing Machinery,* Seattle, October 1977, 227–233.

Green, C. Application of theorem proving to problem solving. *Proceedings of the first International Joint Conference on Artificial Intelligence,* 1969, 219–239.

Miller, M. A structured planning and debugging environment for elementary programming. *International Journal of Man-Machine Studies,* 1979, *11,* 79–95.

Moore, J., & Newell, A. How can Merlin understand. In L. Gregg (Ed.), *Knowledge and Cognition.* Potomac, Md.: Lawrence Erlbaum Associates, 1973.

Norman, D. A., & Bobrow, D. G. On data-limited and resource-limited processes. *Cognitive Psychology*, 1975, *7,* 44–64.

Polya, G. *How to solve it.* New York: Doubleday Anchor Books, 1957.

Sleeman, D. A problem-solving monitor for a deductive reasoning task. *International Journal of Man-Machine Studies,* 1975, *7,* 183–211.

Yob, G. Hunt the Wumpus. *Creative computing,* September/October 1975, 51–54.

6 Problem Solving and Education

Herbert A. Simon
Carnegie-Mellon University

A central design issue, when we are planning learning experiences for our students (otherwise known as curriculum and course planning), is how much and what kinds of transfer of knowledge we can expect from the specific content of textbooks, lectures, and homework problems to the tasks that students will be expected to handle in subsequent courses and in professional life. If we think that basic, broadly transferable knowledge and skills are learnable and teachable, then we will aim our courses at such knowledge and skills, without too much concern for "covering" any specific information, topics, or techniques.

On the other hand, if we believe that the human capability for transfering knowledge and skill from specific situations to analogical but not identical situations is very limited, then we will be much more concerned, in planning courses and curricula, with predicting the exact kinds of problems our students will have to deal with, and with making sure that we "cover" these topics in our course materials.

In view of the enormous change in the world's knowledge that can take place in a student's professional lifetime, and of the constantly growing range of topics for which coverage can plausibly be demanded, it is hard to be optimistic about predicting students' specific future needs for knowledge or skill, or providing adequate coverage in already crowded curricula for a host of specific topics. Our teaching responsibilities urge us to a faith in transfer of training.

EVIDENCE ON TRANSFER

The empirical evidence for the transferability of knowledge and skills to new task situations is very mixed. The belief that students can be taught to "think logically" by offering them courses in Latin or logic was punctured by the celebrated studies of Thorndike in the 1920s (Thorndike, 1924). But Thorndike's research, and other studies in the same genre, did not prove transfer impossible (nor did Thorndike make such claims). They simply showed that certain specific kinds of instruction don't produce transfer. In the past half-century, we have learned a great deal about the conditions that could make it possible.

1. Transfer from Task A to Task B requires that some of the processes or knowledge used in Task B be essentially identical with some of the processes or knowledge that have been learned while acquiring skill in Task A. To take a trivially obvious example, in a college physics course, a student who has previously learned the calculus well will have an easier time solving problems that require the calculus than a student whose calculus skills are shaky. The calculus skills have been transfered to the physics performance because they are used directly in that performance. (Even here, of course, the transfer is not necessarily painless and automatic. The student may possess calculus skills without recognizing that they are applicable to a particular physics problem, or without knowing exactly how to apply them.)

2. To secure substantial transfer of skills acquired in the environment of one task, learners need to be made explicitly aware of these skills, abstracted from their specific task content. (Some of the evidence is reviewed in Woodworth and Schlosberg, 1954, pp.825–830.)

It might, indeed, be possible to teach logical thinking in Latin courses, provided that the students were given tasks in which such thinking was a major component, and provided that the processes of logical thinking that the students were acquiring were made explicit. Whether it would be *efficient* to teach logical thinking in this way is another question.

KNOWLEDGE AND SKILL

Another thing that research on cognitive skills has taught us in recent years is that there is no such thing as expertness without knowledge—extensive and accessible knowledge. No one, no matter how intelligent, skilled in problem solving, or talented, becomes a chess grandmaster without 10 years of intense exposure to the task environment of chess. Hence, in the training of professionals, the problem of coverage cannot be avoided. We cannot produce physicists without teaching physics, or psychologists without teaching psychology. I doubt whether anyone will want to dispute these propositions, but I mention them to qualify any later impression I may create to the effect that I believe that training in problem solving can compensate (at least compensate very far) for ignorance of subject matter.

We are just beginning to get a picture, through research in artificial intelligence and computer simulation of human thinking, of the amounts of knowledge the expert has available—of the size of his or her data bank. For example, the *INTERNIST* system now performs medical diagnoses, over the whole range of internal medicine, at a highly competent professional level (Pople, 1977). *MYCIN* has a similar capability for bacteriological diseases (Shortliffe, 1976). The knowledge stored in the data structures associated with these programs cannot be too dissimilar to the knowledge on these same topics possessed by a good human diagnostician. By constructing artificial-intelligence programs for professional-level tasks, we have acquired similar insights into the knowledge possessed by bank investment officers, by chemists who interpret mass spectrograms, and by professional chess players.

We do not yet have enough information about most of these data bases or the way they are represented in human memory, to provide a numerical measure of their size, in psychologically meaningful units like chunks. However, in one domain, chess, we do actually have a rough quantitative measure. A chess master has to have approximately 50,000 chunks stored in memory just to be able to recognize various configurations of pieces that are encountered repeatedly in games (Simon & Gilmartin, 1973). To explain what that means, I will have to say a little about what a "chunk" is and about the role of recognition memory within the total data structure (Simon, 1974, 1976).

A "chunk" is any perceptual configuration (visual, auditory, or what not) that is familiar and recognizable. For those of us who know the English language, spoken and printed English words are chunks. Even some hackneyed phrases may be stored as chunks: "In union there is strength" is a chunk for most of us. For a person educated in Japanese schools, any one of several thousand Chinese ideograms is a single chunk (and not just a complex collection of lines and squiggles), and even many pairs of such ideograms constitute single chunks. For an experienced chess player, a "fianchettoed castled Black King's position" is a chunk, describing the respective locations of six or seven of the Black pieces.

As a rule of thumb, human short-term memory can hold about four chunks at a time, but long-term memory an unlimited number. However, adding one new chunk to the long-term memory store requires about 8 seconds of attention. Adding a complex chunk that is itself a composite of a number of more elementary chunks may require several minutes, if the elementary chunks have to be acquired at the same time. Hence, even if memorizing activities were perfectly efficient, which they aren't, and if a person spent all his time at them, which he doesn't, acquiring 50,000 chunks would involve a substantial number of hours' application. When we remember that these recognizable patterns are only a fraction—and probably a small fraction—of the total body of knowledge the expert must have available, we see that we can account for a significant part of the 10 years' learning time he needs for acquiring his expertness.

However, if we carry out the arithmetic, it does seem that there are a good many more working hours in the year than are accounted for by this learning, and that we should be able to compress the learning processes by a factor of 10 or more. I shall return to this point later to express some skepticism as to the recoverability of much of this learning time. To anticipate, the 8-second parameter derives mainly from experiments on rote memorization, and memorization may be only a part of what is involved in skill acquisition. Meanwhile, the chunk parameter does provide us with an upper bound on learning rates.

Data on the rates at which schoolchildren are expected to acquire knowledge are consistent with estimates of the sizes of expert data bases. Japanese school children learn about 300 new ideograms per year (for words already known to them in the oral language), together with a substantial number of ideogram pairs. Learning each ideogram also involves learning several more elementary chunks. Reading books for American school children in the elementary grades typically introduce them to about 500 words each year. We made some informal estimates of the number of essential new "facts" that are introduced by each chapter in a college physics textbook and arrived at comparable estimates for a year's course—hundreds of such "facts," each fact involving a constellation of new chunks.

What is the role in the performance of complex tasks of this memory for familiar patterns? We may think of long-term memory as a large indexed and cross-referenced encyclopedia in which the articles are arranged irregularly, so that all information in the text must be accessed directly through the index or indirectly by means of cross-references (Simon, 1976). The familiar patterns are the index entries that enable the user, upon recognition of critical features of the problem situation, to evoke relevant knowledge from the body of the text. A skilled physician recognizes symptoms, which evoke possible courses of treatment. A chessplayer recognizes configurations of pieces, which evoke possible effective moves. An important part of professional skill appears to be embedded in such pairs of recognizable conditions linked to appropriate actions.

In recent years, a number of powerful applied artificial-intelligence programs have been constructed in which the knowledge is almost entirely embedded in such condition-action pairs. The technical AI name for a system using this architecture is *production system* (Newell & Simon, 1972). One of the main advantages claimed, and to some extent demonstrated, for production systems is their extensibility. New knowledge is added to such a system simply by inserting new productions—new text and new index entries to access it. Moreover, the homogeneity of the system facilitates the designing of completely general processes to operate on it. All is not as simple as this sounds; nevertheless, the purported advantages have proved not to be illusory. Production systems today provide both the most promising formalism for applied AI systems that require large data bases, and the most plausible model for human learning of professional subjects.

GENERAL PROBLEM-SOLVING SKILLS

If professional knowledge is largely incorporated in large production systems—in an indexed encyclopedia—one might well wonder what place there is in professional skill for general problem-solving methods, and whether there are any such general methods to be learned or transfered.

Indeed, some rather extravagant statements have appeared in the AI literature that could be interpreted to assert that general methods are unimportant. For example, Goldstein and Papert (1977) have said: "Today there has been a shift in paradigm. The fundamental problem of understanding intelligence is not the identification of a few powerful techniques, but rather the question of how to represent large amounts of knowledge in a fashion that permits their effective use and interactions.

The error in this claim lies in its either-or stance. Two-bladed scissors are still the most effective kind. In addition to the large body of knowledge that is represented in semantically rich systems, there have to be processes for operating on that knowledge to solve problems and answer questions. When the knowledge is incorporated in condition-action pairs, as it is in production systems, these pairs themselves represent processes: When the conditions of such a pair are satisfied, the actions are executed. In a pure production system, then, the general methods are embedded in the productions themselves, in the form taken by the conditions and the actions. If we examine large systems like DENDRAL and MYCIN, we find incorporated in the productions and their organization the standard general-purpose problem-solving techniques of artificial intelligence: for example, the hypothesize-and-test method, means-ends analysis, and best-first search (Feigenbaum, 1977).

Bare facts, however they are stored in memory, do not solve problems. However intimately data and process are intermingled in them, the components of production systems, the individual productions, are processes, not simply pieces of data. And these processes will be effective precisely to the extent that they embody the "few powerful techniques" that Goldstein and Papert dismiss as unimportant.

In addition, most of the large production systems that have been built so far (like the two mentioned previously) are specialized to a particular class of problem-solving tasks, tasks we may describe as taxonomic, using data primarily for purposes of identification. DENDRAL uses mass spectrogram and nuclear magnetic resonance data to identify the molecular species that produced the data. MYCIN uses symptomatic manifestations to identify bacterial diseases. In both cases, the system does what the index of our hypothetical encyclopedia does: It recognizes familiar patterns. And this is just what productions do: recognize when their conditions are satisfied. In systems designed to do other kinds of problem solving, the general methods used, in addition to the production-system architecture itself, are likely to be more conspicuous.

I have commented on this issue at some length because it has important implications for education, in general, and for the topic of my chapter, in particular. If it were true that the storage of properly represented and organized bodies of knowledge were the whole story, then we could return peacefully to our preoccupation with subject-matter content as the main concern in curriculum-building and teaching, and we could give up our efforts to teach general techniques for problem solving that would be transferable from one domain to another.

The evidence from close examination of AI programs that perform professional-level tasks, and the psychological evidence from human transfer experiments, indicate both that powerful general methods do exist and that they can be taught in such a way that they can be used in new domains where they are relevant. We reassert our earlier conclusion that the scissors does indeed have two blades and that effective professional education calls for attention to both subject-matter knowledge and general skills.

LEARNING PROCESSES:
ADAPTIVE PRODUCTION SYSTEMS

Artificial intelligence research on the *performance* of problem-solving tasks is far ahead of research on how problem-solving skills are *acquired*. In spite of the enormous amount of research that has been done in psychology on the topic of learning (mainly within a behaviorist tradition), the amount of knowledge we have about the information processes involved in solving problems is large compared with the very modest amount we have about the information processes involved in learning. Any proposals to teach general problem-solving skills must take account not only of the role such skills play in problem-solving performance but also of what we know about how they can be acquired.

If a problem solver is organized as a production system, a discrete set of condition-action pairs, then learning can occur by the addition of new productions, by the deletion of productions, or by rearrangement of the order in which the conditions of products are tested (Waterman, 1970). Systems that have the capability of modifying production systems automatically in one or more of these ways are called *adaptive production systems* (Rychener et al., 1977). Systems that permit human users to insert, delete, or modify productions interactively are called *instructible production systems.* Adaptive and instructible production systems provide two models of how learning can take place: a self-instruction and a teaching model.

Students learn both by being taught and by self-instruction—in varying mixes for different students. A priori, it might appear that it would obviously be easier to learn with the help of a teacher than by self-instruction. The teacher could simply "provide" the student with the appropriate program—whether organized as a production system or otherwise—which the student could then internalize. This notion rests on what might be called "the fallacy of rote memorization." there is no direct way in which the words pronounced by a teacher can be stored directly as productions available to the student. There must be a conversion of the external language into the internal representation of the student's production system, and neither he nor the teacher know explicitly what that representatin is. Rote memorization, as we know all too well, produces the ability to repeat back the memorized material but not the ability to use it in solving problems.

In the instructible production systems of artificial intelligence, this difficulty can be by-passed, since the way in which information is stored internally is known to the user or the programmer (Feigenbaum, 1977). A simple "front end" can be provided (e.g., the TEIRESIAS front end for MYCIN) that converts productions stated in the user's language (e.g., a subset of English) into productions represented in the programming language (e.g., LISP in the case of MYCIN). In human learning, this conversion program must be provided by the learner.

If we admit this much, then we can see that self-instruction need be no more difficult, and no different in kind, from learning with the help of a teacher. We simply replace the teacher's oral words with the written words of the textbook. Of course I am oversimplifying. The textbook cannot monitor the performance of the student, observe his difficulties, and modify the instruction accordingly.[1] Nevertheless, the processes of converting input language into usable skills must be basically the same in the two cases, and

---

[1]Programmed texts, at their present state of development, can do a little of this but only a trivial amount. A few automated tutorial programs, of which SOPHIE is an example, take several more steps toward simulating the teacher's capabilities.

what we learn about doing the one should be useful in understanding how the other is done.

Our proposed model of a human learner, then, becomes an adaptive production system that can take a textbook as its input and acquire the skills that the textbook is undertaking to teach. At least in scientific and technical subjects, two of the ways in which students learn from textbooks are: (1) examining closely the worked-out examples that the textbook provides; and (2) working the problems at the end of the chapter. Textbooks contain much other material besides worked-out examples and problems, but it is my experience, both as teacher and learner, that these two classes of items occupy a large fraction of the productive learning time.

LEARNING FROM EXAMPLES

Consider the chapter in an algebra textbook that explains how to solve a single linear algebraic equation in one unknown. The first part of the chapter will set out the basic operations that may be performed on an equation without changing its solutions: adding, subtracting, multiplying, or dividing, with the same number on both sides of the equation. Each of these operations will be illustrated by one or more examples. The remainder of the chapter will be devoted to the algorithm for solving a linear equation, using these basic operations. This will mostly be done by example, starting with easy cases and gradually generalizing to more difficult ones.

A clever student, after studying no more than a couple of the examples, will have acquired an algorithm for solving linear equations that will probably be with him for the rest of his life. He may confirm and practice the skill by working problems at the end of the chapter, but the whole process can be over remarkably quickly. Less talented students may follow the same process successfully but less quickly and more painfully (i.e., with more false steps along the way). What can we say about the processes that are going on here?

David Neves (1978) has constructed an adaptive production system that simulates this learning process. Let us suppose that the basic operations for manipulation of equations have already been mastered, and that the system is provided with the following worked-out example:

1. $5X + 2 = 3X + 8$
2. $5X = 3X + 8 - 2$
3. $5X = 3X + 6$
4. $5X - 3X = 6$
5. $2X = 6$
6. $X = 3$

The textbook will usually also supply the information that the second expression was obtained from the first by subtracting 2 from both sides of the equation; the third from the second by combining the numerical terms on the right-hand side; and so on. The system begins by comparing the first two expressions and by noting the differences between them. It notices that the left-hand side has lost a numerical term and that the right-hand side has gained a term. It notes also that the operation performed was to subtract that numerical term from both sides. From these facts, it infers and constructs a new production:

> If there is a numerical term, N, on the left-hand side, then subtract N from both sides.

The same process is followed with the second and third expressions. The production derived here might take the following form:

> If there are two distinct numerical terms on the right-hand side, N and M, say, replace them by their algebraic sum.

The system repeats the process for each successive pair of expressions, producing, in all, five different productions. This set of productions, in their order of discovery, constitute a fairly general system for solving a linear algebraic equation in one unknown, as the reader can verify by hand-simulating its performance with other equations. Hence, having built this system of productions, the system can now solve most of the problems at the end of the textbook chapter.

There are no end of troublesome details I have skipped over in my description of this learning procedure, which makes its execution less trivial than may appear from the example, but I have illustrated the main principles. One "detail," of course, is that the system has to select the appropriate level of generalization in inducing the general rule from the particular numbers and letters that appear in the example.

Let us see what general ideas about learning can be extracted from this example. First, it is clear that the procedure rests on quite general principles that are not restricted in their application to this particular case. The logic of the learning system might be paraphrased as follows:

The solution of an equation is an expression consisting of an X followed by an equals sign followed by a real number. If we are given two expressions, one of which lies closer to this goal than the other along a solution path, find the differences between the two expressions, find the operator that converted the first into the second, and find in the first expression any parameter or parameters used to instantiate the operator. Now create a new production.

The left-hand side should consist of a test for one of the differences that distinguished the first expression from the second, and the difference tested for should contain the parameter mentioned previously. The right-hand side of the production should consist of the operator that converted the first expression into the second, appropriately instantiated. Now change the constants that appear in condition and action of the production into variables of the appropriate types.

LEARNING BY DOING

Anyone familiar with problem-solving systems like the General Problem Solver (GPS) will recognize the logic of the system as an application of means-ends analysis (Newell & Simon, 1972). We have a certain situation (the first expression of a pair); we want a different situation (the second expression). We detect a difference between the two situations, and we search memory for an operator that is relevant for reducing differences of this kind. We apply the operator and examine the resulting expression to see if the difference has been removed. (In the case of the worked-out example, a successful outcome is guaranteed.) This is a particularly simple case of means-ends analysis, because only a single application of a single operator is needed to produce the result; hence, there is no danger that the system will embroil itself in a large search for the answer. This is precisely the point in exhibiting all the intermediate steps in the example. Of course, this can be done at various levels of detail. For example, in the instance we have used, it may be assumed that the student will always simplify expressions "automatically" (i.e., that each arithmetic operation in an equation will include the subsequent simplification step) so that expressions (2) and (4) need not be exhibited.

Omitting the low-level details suggests the next step of generalization. Even if only expressions (1) and (6) were exhibited, the logic of the program would still apply. In fact, we would not need the exact detail of expression (6), but only its form: an expression consisting of X followed by equals followed by a real number. Then a GPS-like adaptive production system could still construct a set of productions for solving algebraic equations by successively removing a whole set of differences between (1) and (6), and not just a single difference. This might require some search and some guidance of that search; hence, the adaptive GPS would have to have a few additional capabilities in addition to those possessed by the system that always had a worked-out example available.

We may view the adaptive GPS in a slightly different way (Anzai & Simon, 1979). Suppose that we have a quite flexible and general problem-solving system, which depends mainly on selective search and means–ends analysis to solve problems. It probably will not be very powerful in any particular problem domain, relying as it does on weak general methods. However, it may be able to work its way, by brute force and awkwardness, through problems in some domains that are new to it. Having found at least one solution in this way, it can ignore the various false trails it followed in its search and can focus its attention on the successful solution path. But this solution path is precisely a worked-out example, and the same procedures that were used to build a production system from such an example can be applied to it.

Finally, there are situations in which the adaptive GPS can succeed even though it cannot initially find a problem solution. It may be able to detect when it has made some progress toward a solution or, alternatively, when it is searching ineffectively (e.g., when it has gone around a loop). Then, it can create new productions that exploit its progress or avoid its inefficient behaviors. These new productions may increase the efficiency of its search until it can solve the problem—at which point we are reduced to the case of the worked-out example. Anzai and Simon have constructed a system that is capable of learning to solve the Tower of Hanoi problem in an efficient way, starting only with general problem-solving procedures of the kind just indicated, together with adaptive means for profiting from its progress and its errors.

LESSONS FOR INSTRUCTION

What lessons may we plausibly draw from these experiments? First, the adaptive production systems I have described provide an explanation of how learning from worked-out examples and from problems can take place. Second, they show that means-ends analysis, a central component of general problem-solving processes, plays a crucial role in learning. Hence, they give us some further insight into the respective roles of general skills and special knowledge in achieving high-level performance.

If our account is basically correct, then general skills (e.g., means–ends analysis) will be particularly important in the learning stages but will also show up implicitly in the *form* of the productions that are used in the skilled performance. The production system we have sketched for solving algebraic equations is a specialized instantiation of the general means–ends schema. Aside from their embodiment in specialized productions, general problem-solving techniques may not be evident in the professional's skilled behavior when he is engaged in relatively familiar tasks. They are likely to play an essential role whenever he has to move into new territory and attempt new learning.

The experiment also contains an important lesson for teachers and the writers of textbooks—a lesson that may be stated in terms of the classical dichotomy between rote learning and meaningful learning. Or perhaps I should call it a "hypothesis" rather than a lesson. It is a rule of algebra that you may subtract the same expression from both sides of an equation. The rule gives no hint of the circumstances under which a problem solver should avail himself of that privilege. The production system derived from the worked-out example gives exactly that kind of advice. It says that, if the goal is to solve the equation for X, and if there is a numerical constant on the left-hand side of the equation, the subtraction rule should be used to remove the constant. If you will examine some typical algebra textbooks, you will find that all of them make the rule of addition completely explicit, but you will almost surely find, also, that the *conditional* rule, which tells when the operation is appropriately applied, is only implicit or, if mentioned, is not much emphasized or elaborated.

This is not an isolated case. Generally speaking, textbooks are much more explicit in enunciating the laws of mathematics or of nature than in saying anything about when these laws may be useful in solving problems. The actions of the productions needed to solve problems in the domain of the textbooks are laid out systematically, but they are not securely connected with the conditions that should evoke them. It is left largely to the student (by examining worked-out examples, by working problems, or in some other way) to generate the productions, the condition-action pairs, that are required to solve problems. Hence, if the student mainly memorizes, learns by rote, the laws stated in the textbook, he or she will acquire little or no problem-solving ability.

We can see the same thing in diagnostic skills as in more general kinds of problem-solving skills. A physician needs to know how to go about treating the various diseases he may encounter in his patients. But that knowledge is of no use to him unless it is evoked by the presence of the appropriate symptoms. A large part of his medical knowledge has the form of condition-action pairs, in which the symptoms of disease are the conditions, and in which the treatments associated with the corresponding disease entities are the actions. On the basis of casual examination of textbooks in medicine and in various branches of taxonomic biology, I gather the impression that there is somewhat more attention given to expressing knowledge in these fields in the form of productions than there is in branches of science that are largely concerned with the exposition of natural laws.

Of course, I expect that productions, statements of the relation between conditions and recommended actions, can also be learned by rote—that is, by learning the verbal rules without acquiring the ability actually to perform the tests incorporated in the conditions. I am not suggesting that making the condition sides of our productions explicit provides any royal road to learning.

TEACHING PROBLEM SOLVING

The lessons for pedagogy that can be extracted from my remarks are clear enough that they don't need to be explicated at great length. A first lesson is that we can best think of most skills—both general skills and competence in specific subject matter—as being represented in productions rather than propositions. If this is true, then we need to teach our students that this *is* the form that most professional knowledge takes, so that they can monitor their own learning more effectively and not mistake learning propositions for acquiring basic skills. I continue to encounter many students who do not really know the difference between rote learning and learning with understanding, and who wonder why, after they have memorized some material with great thoroughness, they cannot pass examinations that require them to solve problems.

Second, there is a small arsenal of general problem-solving procedures that have been identified from research in psychology and artificial intelligence. In this chapter, I have particularly stressed one of them—means-ends analysis. Since we know that skills will be transfered only when the principles on which they rest are made explicit, these procedures need to be made evident for students, and then they need to be practiced, and practiced again. We are engaged here not merely in knowledge acquisition but in skill acquisition. All of our experiences tell us that people do not learn to ride bicycles simply by having the principles explained to them. What they must mostly do is to ride them. Similarly, the active practice of problem solving, but problem solving with awareness, should be the main core of a problem-solving course, or of problem-solving instruction in a subject-matter course.

Third, a considerable part of the training in problem solving *can* profitably take place in subject-matter courses. This has two advantages. First, it facilitates the transfer of skills that have been learned outside the subject-matter context. Second, it permits attention to be given to the whole continuum of skills, from the most general to the most specific technique, without focusing on just a single part of the spectrum. I think that at Carnegie-Mellon University, some of the most effective training in problem solving that has been done over the years has been carried out in engineering analysis courses within the Engineering College. In courses like these, students learn not only how to use means-ends analysis, or functional analysis, but also how to analyze a wide range of situations in terms of broad physical principles like conservation of energy.

Fourth, instruction in problem solving should place a considerable emphasis upon such techniques of self-instruction as learning from worked-out examples and learning by working problems; for it is precisely in the context of such learning situations that the student's general problem-solving techniques, as distinct from his special skills, are called upon most heavily. Such instruction will also help to alert students to the ways in which general techniques are embedded implicitly in the formats of the productions that carry their special knowledge.

Finally, the perceptual aspects of skill probably deserve increased emphasis. I have suggested that, in our textbooks and in our teaching, we tend to underemphasize the condition sides of the condition–action pairs. We need to help our students improve their skills of recognition and to help them acquire techniques for exercising those skills, so that if they have learned what to do, they will not be slow in recognizing when to do it.

Many of the points I have been making are familiar enough in current ways of teaching problem solving. From Polya down to recent textbooks, we have emphasized the working of examples and the explication of problem-solving principles. My emphasis upon perceptual skills, and upon the application of problem-solving to self-instructional tasks, are perhaps more novel. In any case, we are unlikely to find idle time on our own or our students' hands in either the general course on problem solving or in more special courses that try to teach problem-solving skills in a subject-matter context.

CONCLUSION

After entering all of the appropriate caveats about transfer, and after taking account of the essentiality of specialized knowledge for skilled professional performance, I believe that a strong case can still be made for teaching problem solving explicitly, as an important component of professional education. It must be taught, of course, in the context of a rich environment of problems—mostly but not entirely drawn from the professional field in question.

In teaching problem solving, major emphasis needs to be directed toward extracting, making explicit, and practicing problem-solving heuristics—both general heuristics, like means—ends analysis, and more specific heuristics, like applying the energy-conservation principle in physics. It is desirable for students to become aware of how heuristics are organized in memory, as sets of productions that provide not only a repertory of problem-solving actions but also conditions, associated with these, that serve to index the actions and to evoke them when they need to be used. A student's own learning processes will be enhanced if he understands that a large part of his professional skill resides in the ability to recognize rapidly the situational cues that signal the appropriateness of particular actions. In this learning, he needs to pay specific attention to the acquisition of these recognition skills.

A major goal in teaching problem solving should be to help the student acquire skills of self-instruction. In examining these skills in the context of recent AI research on learning, we see that they are intimately bound up with general problem-solving skills. Self-instruction involves being able to learn from worked-out examples and by working textbook problems. Doing this employs means–ends analysis, and the production systems that evolve during such learning embody means–ends analysis implicitly.

There is some empirical evidence that problem-solving skills can be taught, although there is regrettably little evidence that such instruction is cost-effective, as compared with equal effort devoted to subject-matter skills. As an empirical scientist, I could wish that the evidence were stronger. As a practical teacher, I am satisfied that, as we continue to learn more about the nature of problem-solving processes, we will be able to teach general problem-solving skills with increasing effectiveness and be able to circumvent the unsolvable problems of coverage and of predicting what specific knowledge our students will need 30 years hence.

ACKNOWLEDGMENT

This research was supported by Research Grant MH-07722 from the National Institute of Mental Health.

REFERENCES

Anzai, Y., & Simon, H. A. Strategy transformations in problem-solving: A case study. *Psychological Review,* 1979, in press.

Feigenbaum, E. A. The art of artificial intelligence: Themes and case studies of knowledge engineering. *Proceedings of the Fifth International Joint Conference on Artificial Intelligence,* Pittsburgh, Pa.: Department of Computer Science, Carnegie-Mellon University, 1977.

Goldstein, I., & Papert, S. Artificial intelligence, language, and the study of knowledge, *Cognitive Science,* 1977, *1,* 84-124.

Neves, D. M. A computer program that learns algebraic procedures by examining examples and by working problems in a textbook. *Proceedings of the Second National Conference of the Canadian Society for Computational Studies of Intelligence,* 1978.

Newell, A., & Simon, H. A. *Human problem solving.* Englewood Cliffs, N.J.: Prentice-Hall, 1972.

Pople, H. Problem solving: An exercise in synthetic reasoning. *Proceedings of the Fifth International Joint Conference on Artificial Intelligence,* Pittsburgh, Pa.: Computer Science Department, Carnegie-Mellon University, 1977.

Rychener, M., et al. Problems in building an instructible production system. *Proceedings of the Fifth International Joint Conference on Artificial Intelligence.* Pittsburgh, Pa.: Computer Science Department, Carnegie-Mellon University, 1977.

Shortliffe, E. *Computer-based medical consultations: MYCIN.* New York: Elsevier, 1976.

Simon, H. A. How big is a chunk? *Science,* 1974, *183,* 482-488.

Simon, H. A. The information-storage system called "human memory." In M. R. Rosenzeig & E. L. Bennett (Eds.), *Neural mechanisms of learning and memory*. Cambridge, Mass.: MIT Press, 1976.

Simon, H. A., & Gilmartin, K. A simulation of memory for chess positions. *Cognitive Psychology*, 1973, *5*, 29–46.

Thorndike, E. L. Mental discipline in high school studies, *Journal of Educational Psychology*, 1924, *15*, 1–22; 83–98.

Waterman, D. Generalization learning techniques for automating the learning of heuristics. *Artificial Intelligence*, 1970, *1*, 121–170.

Woodworth, R. S., & Schlosberg, H. *Experimental psychology* (2nd ed.). New York: Holt, Rinehart & Winston, 1954.

7 Cognitive Engineering and Education

Donald A. Norman
University of California, San Diego

It is strange that we expect students to learn yet seldom teach them anything about learning. We expect students to solve problems yet seldom teach them about problem solving. And, similarly, we sometimes require students to remember a considerable body of material yet seldom teach them the art of memory. It is time we made up for this lack, time that we developed the applied disciplines of learning and problem solving and memory. We need to develop the general principles of how to learn, how to remember, how to solve problems, and then to develop applied courses, and then to establish the place of these methods in an academic curriculum.

I have been asked to comment upon two chapters, one by Herbert Simon, the other by Ira Goldstein. The two chapters differ considerably, the one talking of the need for general instruction in problem-solving skills, the other demonstrating a new technological development in automated instruction. I find both chapters important, for combined they point toward a discipline of "cognitive engineering": the development of a systematic corpus of knowledge and of techniques about cognitive processes. The techniques under discussion in this symposium all deal with the problems of learning and teaching. But the principles go beyond these two applications. The principles speak of a need for a discipline that can develop applied techniques, that combine our increasing knowledge of human cognition with advances in technology in order to produce new applications for learning, for teaching, and for design, in general.

COGNITIVE ENGINEERING

What does it mean to have a discipline of "cognitive engineering"? One thing is that there should exist a solid, substantiated body of principles that have been shown to be useful: principles for solving problems, principles for learning, principles for remembering. These are the tools of the discipline, and they can and should be applied to specific content areas, much as applied mathematics is both developed and taught in general, and applied to specific areas of application. Before we can establish an area of "cognitive engineering", we need to develop the concepts and techniques of the field, to perform explicit studies of the teaching of problem solving, of learning, of memory. These studies should concentrate upon practical aspects of these topics. Good approximate models of psychological functioning will suffice to develop good applied methods of learning and problem solving: We need not wait till all the theoretical dust has settled down within the technical journals. However, as the papers in this conference demonstrate, we already have considerable knowledge that can be taught, that will give general, powerful techniques for improving one's performance at problem solving, at learning, and at memory. Indeed, the learning of memory skills is a good case in point. Although we still do not understand the theoretical structure of memory, efficient and practical methods for remembering material have been known for hundreds of years but almost never taught in schools. Medical students bootleg the mnemonic techniques for learning the anatomical names, because their instructors seldom will admit they exist (nor will the textbooks), despite the fact that the instructors and textbook writers probably used these very same methods themselves.

The establishment of a "cognitive engineering" for the teaching of problem solving would seem to require several steps:

1. To understand enough about the psychology of learning or of problem solving that applied techniques can be developed (we may already be at this stage);
2. To develop applied methods and formal courses in these methods that can aid in the general problem-solving and learning abilities of our students (we are far from reaching this point);
3. To use this knowledge in two ways:
   a. To develop courses in the methods of learning, of problem solving, of remembering to provide students with important cognitive tools.
   b. To develop better instructional systems for teaching, improving upon conventional teaching and developing useful innovations, and (perhaps most valuable) to make use of new technological developments and new techniques of cognitive science to make interactive, intelligent tutoring systems a reality.

4. To demonstrate the effectiveness of these techniques and to gain sufficient academic and public acceptance that they will not only be taught, but that they will be sought after, and that research and teaching on these topics will be seen as virtuous and important.

The area of memory has passed through Steps 1 and 2, but the teaching of memory skills fails at Step 3. Courses in "how to remember" are not considered academically sound. People who do research on memory aids are not full-fledged members of the research community. And, as in the case of medicine, even if the instructor of a course uses the techniques personally, it isn't considered proper to take the time to teach them.

Folk Psychology

Everyone has their own model of how the mind works, a model that has been developed over a lifetime of experience. Some aspects of the model are determined by our culture, as our vocabulary makes use of implicit models of mind. These models of mind I call "folk psychology." They play important roles in governing how we do things, how we learn, how we study, and how we interact with others and the world. The people who claim to be unable to "do" mathematics have a model of themselves and of the requirements of mathematics and claim the requirements to be incompatible.

Folk knowledge is often very useful, supplying practical rules that serve us well in applications, even if erroneous. I have found that a common belief of "folk physics" is that a vacuum "sucks" things like air, water, and loose objects toward itself. ("Nature abhors a vacuum.") This bit of "folk physics" is perfectly workable, and it is useful in understanding how a straw works, what happens when a television picture tube breaks, and so on. I need not explain to this audience that it is a dangerous sort of knowledge, leading to erroneous notions. It is also incomplete knowledge, for of the several people that I have interviewed that had this belief, none could quite explain a mechanism for the "sucking."

I contend that "folk psychology" is just as inaccurate and misleading as "folk" anything, that people's models of how their minds work are apt to be wrong and, worse, misleading. Many adults believe that the best way to learn something is to say it over and over again—rehearsal—yet many studies have demonstrated that this is one of the worst possible techniques to use. People's beliefs about their abilities may be based on erroneous information, but those beliefs will then control their activities, thereby proving the belief: The person who claims to be constitutionally incapable of learning mathematics is probably incapable of learning mathematics, at least while that belief is still held.

"Cognitive engineering" must replace "folk psychology" with "cognitive psychology," with a useful model of mind that can be used by their possessors to guide them in useful pursuits.

This Conference, and the Chapters by Simon and Goldstein

There are two aims of this conference, according to its organizers, Reif and Tuma: "to encourage the teaching of generally useful problem-solving skills and to provide the know-how whereby such teaching can effectively be achieved." The two speakers on whom I am asked to comment have neatly divided themselves between these two aims: Simon argues the need for general instruction in problem-solving, coupled, of course, with specific knowledge of topic areas. Goldstein suggests an exciting new use of technological aids to provide the teaching of problem-solving skills, individually guided by a computer coach that understands the structure of the material to be taught, as well as the procedures that should be used by the student. Together, the two chapters complement one another and serve to cover the topic matter of the entire conference.

SIMON'S PROBLEM SOLVING AND LEARNING

In his chapter, Simon urges us to teach problem solving "as an important component of professional education." The techniques are general, he argues, applicable to a wide variety of topics, if only students would be aware of them. The techniques should of course be taught "in the context of a rich environment of problems—mostly but not entirely drawn from the professional field in question." His claim is that there are general skills that need to be taught, skills that would be invaluable for a range of problems in a range of disciplines, and skills that are not now being taught.

Simon has done more than point to this need. He has been one of the primary contributors to our general arsenal of problem-solving tools. Our knowledge of the heuristic rules useful in problem solving, of the power of means–ends analysis, of the techniques that people actually use in solving problems is primarily a result of the work by Simon and his colleagues at Carnegie-Mellon University. Simon's (and Newell's) work has been important in developing our understanding of problem solving. If it has not been useful in the general way that he has advocated in his chapter, it is because the emphasis till now has been on Step 1 of my four-step list: toward developing the theoretical structures of human psychology.

I agree with the major points of the chapter. Where I disagree is in some of the details, but even these disagreements are of the sort that we both support:

They are disagreements that can be resolved by appropriate observations of human behavior. They are the sort of disagreements that will lead toward the major goal of a "cognitive engineering." My major points of disagreement come from two issues: "strength of statement" and "organization of knowledge."

Strength of Statement

I do not believe we yet know enough to make strong statements about what ought to be or ought not to be included in a course on general problem-solving methods. Although there are some general methods that could be of use in general situations, I suspect that in most real situations it is the main specific knowledge that is most relevant. To quote from a statement made in this symposium by Greeno: "General problem-solving methods are of primary use when you do *not* know much." The conclusion I drew from Greeno's talk was that to teach people to be successful in their domain, teach them that domain.

I think students do not have a legitimate "folk psychology." They do not know enough about how to study, or how to learn, or how to solve problems in general. I am sure that general problem-solving skills are essential and that they could be taught. I agree with Simon that they ought to be taught, but what I do not yet know is what the appropriate mix of general and specific knowledge structures ought to be.

Organization of Knowledge

The number of things that we know is large, very large. Not only is it not clear how to estimate the number of things, but is is not quite clear what a "thing" is. Still, the estimates that Simon and his colleagues have made are suggestive. He suggests that a master chess player may know 50,000 "facts" (board configurations) about the game.

I believe that the number "50,000" is a reasonable approximation. I tried the following exercise on myself in an attempt to estimate the amount of my knowledge in one of the domains in which I am reasonably knowledgeable: cooking. I went through the book entitled *Kitchen Wisdom* (Arkin, 1977), 260 pages of "facts," each fact consisting of a hint about kitchen preparation techniques. I estimated that the book had approximately 2600 of these facts and that I knew at least that many myself. (For every statement in the book that I did not know, I could think of one similar statement that was not included in the book.) Each statement actually consisted of several related things that fit together under one useful hint. Therefore, I estimate that the 2600 statements really is something like 10,000 facts. Using this book as a quick estimate of my own knowledge of kitchen techniques, I see that I have about 10,000. Moreover, the book did not cover anything about cooking itself, simply about preparation. I think it would not be too far wrong to say that I have approximately five such collections of knowledge about different aspects of cooking, easily yielding a data base of 50,000 facts about cooking.

Despite the difficulties of estimating what a "fact" should be, I find it not unreasonable to suppose that an expert at a topic knows something like 50,000 things about that topic. The next question is, on how many topics are we expert? More than you might think. We are experts about our own bodies; personal idiosyncracies; about the spatial arrangements of our homes, yards, and environment; the physical characteristics of our house and furniture; the paths to and from frequently traveled locations; and perhaps even the topic matter on which we study and work. We are all experts in at least one language, and as countless theses on natural language processing have rediscovered, in order to understand even simple stories, we must bring to bear a large amount of general world knowledge about the workings of things and the ways of the world.

All of this is to say that we know a lot, and that it is my firm belief that the organization of that lot is the critical aspect of our memory structures. Simon tends to minimize the role of appropriate organization in memory, and I feel this minimization is in error. The general organizational structure that he proposes is that of a production system, a set of rules in condition-action format. I do not think this will suffice.

Production Systems.   Followers of psychology are amused to note that the new tool in cognitive psychology is a rediscovery and formalization of S–R psychology. Internal Ss and internal Rs: made legitimate by the power of computer technology. A production system, let me emphasize, is a powerful tool. Appropriately defined, a production system has all the power of the general Turing machine, and so whatever can be computed, can be computed through production systems. The identification with S–R psychology is not meant to belittle the accomplishment, for what is important in today's approach is the combination of sufficient processing structure and complete specification of the production rules to give formal realization of the power of these systems.

The thing that bothers me is the lack of organization of knowledge. I believe that no real system can long survive without an appropriate organization. Studies of human memory emphasize over and over again the need for proper organization. Simon believes it can all be done by appropriate specialization of the conditional side of a production. In principle, Simon is correct about the theoretical power of the production system. But I am sceptical of the practical power. So far there has never really been a system built that taxes the organizational principles, a system that is expert on many topics—the case that is true of humans. Technological systems of today are small. We will not know about the role of organization until we have more experience. Still, were I designing a course on general learning and general problem-solving skills, I would include a hefty dose of instruction and practice on acquiring appropriate organizational structures within memory.

Summary of the Review of Simon's Chapter

I agree with Simon's main points, with his plea for more study of the teaching of general problem-solving techniques. I am a bit less optimistic than he that we yet know the appropriate things to teach, and I believe that he has slighted the complexity of learning and the need for appropriate organization of knowledge. But let me emphasize that these are simply alternate opinions, not at all in opposition to the major points made by Simon. We need a cognitive engineering for the teaching of problem solving.

GOLDSTEIN'S GENETIC EPISTEMOLOGY

There is a new approach to automated teaching in the air, one that promises some useful developments for the learning of both conventional subject matters and also of the new wave of automated systems that are about to engulf us—text editors, complex games, learning games, computer-assisted everything. The general approach is that of a computer tutor or coach, a nonintrusive, supportive coach who watches over the shoulder of the learner, knowledgeable in both the task to be learned and the current state of knowledge of the learner, intervening now and then to suggest, prod, or clarify. In this chapter, Goldstein proposes one such system, with illustrations of the general features and properties that will be required if these systems are to become more than laboratory exercises. I think that Goldstein's work promises an exciting new future in educational technology: interactive games that entertain while they instruct, teaching fundamental principles and providing general experience and practice, all the while hiding under the cloak of innocent enjoyment.

The general ideas contain some interesting engineering. The important characteristics are that the computer tutor:

- Understands the task and the topic matter.
- Has a model of the student.
- Has knowledge of teaching strategies.
- Uses the task as a medium to teach essential princples.
- Is independent of the task and learning situations, so that occasional failures of the tutoring system have minimal disruptive effect.

The Engineering of Tutoring Systems

In designing an educational tutoring system that will actually be used (as opposed to one that is designed to test or help discover some basic theoretical principles), a number of engineering judgments must be made. The game of Wumpus, together with the computer coach, demonstrates several technological innovations. I believe that Goldstein has provided us with a very important piece of cognitive engineering in the spirit that will characterize the best of the possible new instructional systems. Basically, what we see illustrated is a game that can capture the interest of the young student while incidentally teaching some important principles. To the designer, of course, all the effort has gone into the "incidental" aspects. To the student, however, the game is an enjoyable pursuit, and if there is learning along the way, it comes with the proper motivation, for it leads to improved performance in the situation.

The theme is that of a coach, watching over the student, making comments where appropriate. The hope is that the coach has a good knowledge of both the topic matter and of the student, so the comments can be tailored specifically for the style most effective for this particular student. In practice, however, not enough is known yet about how this can be done. But that is one of the goals of the research.

Goldstein wrote his chapter with historical emphasis. This makes my task more difficult, for it implies that what I do not like now may change later. Nonetheless, there are several things I do not like about the system, things I believe are fundamental to the approach being used and that may not easily be correctible without a reasonably major change in direction. My major difficulties come from two different issues: The first is how well the technique generalizes to other topics; the second is my feeling that Goldstein has oversimplified the analysis of learning.

Generalizability of Topic

The general technique used by Goldstein is that of the "genetic" graph, which allows one to perform an "evolving representation of the problem." I feel this leads to difficulties for several reasons. First, it requires exhaustive analysis of the possible rules structures and histories that a student may pursue. I believe that, for more complex topics, this technique would require such enormous effort and analysis, such complete understanding of the topic, that it would be completely unfeasible. Not only is the amount of effort enormous, but I fear that for many topics we do not have sufficient understanding.

The second difficulty is that it might not be possible, not even in principle, to lay out all the possible paths that a student may take. This appears to be at the basis of the genetic approach. Now, it is true that Goldstein does not require that a student rigidly follow a continuous path through the learning states. It is possible for a student to jump, to make apparent discontinuities in learning. But I see this mechanism as an afterthought, one that tends to violate the spirit of the learning model being proposed.

What is the solution? The very nature of the coaching scheme being proposed by Goldstein relies heavily upon an understanding of where the student is and what the possible new routes can be. I think it should be possible to do away with the elaborate graph of possibilities. I think that by sufficient understanding of the major components that are to be acquired during the task, coupled with an understanding of those components—which includes a statement of prerequisite knowledge—then it should be possible to use the general principles to generate the current state of knowledge of the student and the appropriate direction that should be followed to get the student to the desired state. Alas, my statement is but a vague hope, based upon intuitions and a certain amount of experimentation and thought but not upon any successful application of the technique to any large-scale knowledge. I am not sure exactly what the solution to the problem is, but I do not see how the technique used in the game of Wumpus will generate to larger-scale topics.

Simplification of Learning

Goldstein has emphasized only one aspect of learning: "the problem of forming appropriate structures." My colleagues find that there is more to learning than this; a considerable amount of information must occur (accretion), and there must be sufficient practice and experience with concepts that they become automated, removed from the need for large amounts of mental computation in order that they be used (tuning).

Students are not passive learners. They are not simple receptacles for the new knowledge imparted by the teacher. They squirm and struggle. The knowledge that they are learning must make sense to them. The studies that have been conducted in my laboratory indicate that students strive to interpret what is being presented to them. We are fond of quoting the "iceberg phenomenon": What the student gets from the instructor or the textbook is but the tip of the iceberg. The student then constructs a huge substructure to support that tip. But a student is much like a theorist, constructing grand structures from partial knowledge, searching for confirmatory evidence, ignoring that which does not fit. I fear that instruction is more complex than addressed by Goldstein (or, for that matter, by Simon). (An introduction to this approach is given in Bott, 1978, and Norman, 1979.)

We find that knowledge builds upon knowledge. The manner of the building and the nature of the framework depend on the student's interpretation of what is being learned. Start wrong, and the student may never recover. Students use prior knowledge, analogies to other topics, and metaphors.

The students appear to build new knowledge structures through analogy to some conceptual models. If there is no conceptual model provided, the student blithely makes one up. We have found it critical that the instructor be the one to provide the model. So, one of the critical aspects of teaching appears to be in providing an appropriate conceptual model for the student.

Finally, my favorite sentence about the nature of learning is: "Learning is not a unitary activity" (Rumelhart & Norman, 1978). We have found it useful to identify three different types of learning: accretion, structuring, and tuning. But I am now going beyond my purpose: I am starting to carry on. Let me conclude with a summary.

SUMMARY

The chapters by Simon and Goldstein offer us some glimpses of new directions in teaching, in learning, in research. It should be possible to teach students about general problem-solving techniques. It should be possible to devise techniques for teaching that generalize far beyond the problem at hand. It should be possible to devise interactive computer systems that watch over performance and offer useful hints and suggestions, systems that act as friendly coaches and guides for the acquisition of knowledge. The chapters I have been discussing tell us about some ways of moving in these directions.

Simon suggests the teaching of general problem-solving techniques, mixed with particular knowledge about the topic areas for which the techniques are to be applied. Goldstein demonstrates a working computer system that instructs, but pleasantly and naturally, by acting as a coach looking over the shoulder of the student who is engaged in playing a particular game, learning all the while. I see these two chapters as complementary, offering suggestions about new topics and new methods for teaching.

Before these suggestions can be applied in any real settings, considerable engineering development must take place—not hardware engineering, but "cognitive engineering." The techniques must be assessed for their utility and practicality with real students. Some experiments need to be done to determine just how useful instruction in general techniques turns out to be, and just what the appropriate set of techniques ought to be. Considerable experience is needed in the test of actual systems to ensure that they are sufficiently complete and robust for actual use. I suspect that considerable work is needed to translate Simon's pleas for general instruction in problem-solving methods into actual course material. I also suspect that considerable development work must be done with computer systems of the sort discussed by Goldstein before they are capable of working with real students in real environments, and with more complex course material than games like Wumpus. I believe that the necessary development can be done in the applied laboratories of a discipline of "cognitive engineering": They can be moved from the pure research environment in which they have been developed.

The discipline of "cognitive engineering" does not exist. T'is a pity. I suspect there are several areas in which knowledge of cognitive functioning could be applied, if only sufficient developmental work were performed. Almost any situation in which the human mind is a relevant part of the system coul use a systematic engineering application of the lessons from the cognitive sciences. The topics examined in this symposium are only some examples of many that could potentially be of value. We need those applications. But before we can get them, we must have some systematic effort at developing the methods. We need a discipline of "cognitive engineering."

ACKNOWLEDGMENTS

Partial research support was provided by a contract from the Office of Naval Research and the Advanced Research Projects Agency, monitored by ONR under contract N0014-76-C-0628. Support was also provided by National Institutes of Mental Health Grant No. MH-15828-09 to the Center for Human Information Processing.

REFERENCES

Arkin, F. *Kitchen wisdom*. New York: Holt, Rinehart & Winston, 1977.

Bott, R. *A study of complex learning: Theory and methodologies*. Unpublished doctoral dissertation, University of California, San Diego, 1978.

Norman, D. A. What goes on in the mind of the learner? In W. J. McKeachie (Ed.), *Cognition, college teaching, and student learning*, San Francisco: Jossey-Bass, 1979, in press.

Rumelhart, D. E., & Norman, D. A. Accretion, tuning and restructuring: Three modes of learning. In J. W. Cotton & R. Klatsky (Eds.), *Semantic factors in cognition*. Hillsdale, N.J.: Lawrence Erlbaum Associates, 1978.

III TEACHING

8 Teaching Problem Solving in Physics: The Psychological Laboratory and the Practical Classroom

Jill H. Larkin
University of California, Berkeley

As the title of this chapter suggests, I think there is a particularly fruitful interaction between a psychological laboratory, in which the task is to understand the mechanisms of problem solving, and the practical classroom, in which the task is to teach effective problem solving. These two arenas are beginning to have a symbiotic relationship in which the assets of each are brought to bear on the liabilities of the other. In this chapter, I first discuss the mechanisms of this relationship and then illustrate its fruitfulness by discussing a variety of intriguing research occurring as part of this interaction.

Throughout this discussion, I emphasize work on problem solving in mathematics and science, particularly physics, and particularly at the university level. The reasons for this emphasis are the following. First, it is the work I know best, and it provides a coherent set of examples for what I want to say. Second, mathematics and physical sciences, as usually taught at the university level, are particularly structured domains, tightly organized around a relatively few broadly applicable principles. As I shall discuss shortly, such structured domains are particularly attractive arenas for work on problem solving. However, most of the comments I have to make are almost certainly relevant to disciplines other than physics, and some are certainly relevant to disciplines other than mathematics and science.

What then are the major assets and liabilities of work on problem solving in the classroom and in the laboratory, and how do these assets and liabilities relate to each other? Turning first to the classroom, I see three major areas of difficulty.

First, it just seems to be very hard to teach people to solve problems. When instruction is designed with systematic care, it is possible to reliably teach apparently simpler skills such as factual recall, concept identification, or applying algorithms. But when it comes to teaching problem solving, even the best teachers, using considerable accumulated experience, often have limited success.

The difficulty of teaching problem solving is particularly evident in the disciplines I'm considering—mathematics and sciences. This difficulty is due, doubtless in part, to the fact that in these disciplines there are well-defined criteria for successful problem solutions. Thus it is easy to recognize students who can't solve problems adequately. But it may also be that formal, logical problems are intrinsically more difficult than other problems [e.g., problems requiring use of language (writing an essay) or reasoning about human actions (discussing the strategy of the Civil War)]. Perhaps some skills (such as language) are naturally acquired through ordinary experience, whereas other skills (such as the logical skill or constructing a geometry proof) are not acquired in this way.

Whatever the mechanisms of their difficulty, problems in mathematics and science are very hard for many students. Thus teaching students to solve such problems flexibly and skillfully is a particular challenge to anyone seriously concerned with good education for students who live in an increasingly technological society.

A second source of difficulty in work on problem solving in the practical classroom is the relatively little useful input from educational research. The reason is that the research methodologies used most commonly in education are unsuited to providing information about the mechanisms of effective problem solving. Traditionally, educational research has used over-whelmingly the paradigm of the agricultural field study. Some students are given Type X instruction, whereas others are given Type Y; and at the end, differences between their abilities are assessed by statistical comparisons of test-score distributions. Such experiments (when done well) may provide useful assesments of existing instructional programs. But they do not provide good insights into the processes of effective problem solving, the manner in which these processes are acquired, or the kinds of defects that unskillful problem solvers experience. It is this kind of information about mechanisms of problem solving that could be used directly in designing effective instruction.

Despite these difficulties, however, there certainly are individuals who do seem to teach problem solving effectively. For example, a program developed and extensively evaluated by Bloom and Broder (1950) markedly improved college students' chances of doing well on a problem-oriented comprehensive examination. More recent efforts include those of Bauman and Whimbey (Bauman, 1978; Whimbey & Whimbey, 1978), whose students show reliably increased scores on various standardized tests of reasoning and problem solving. Others, such as Lochhead and Woods (Lochhead, 1978; Woods,

1976), are restructuring entire curricula in efforts to enhance students' abilities in solving problems in physics and engineering. The advantages of these programs are clear and considerable. First, these programs do seem to have appreciable benefits for the students they involve. Second, the individuals designing these programs often have done considerable (although informal) analysis of the component skills required for successful problem solving in their discipline. Furthermore, these analyses are not armchair efforts; rather, they are based on extensive observations of students who are acquiring (or failing to acquire) these skills. Thus these individuals who are developing practical instruction in problem solving can be gold mines of intuitive ideas about the important mechanisms of problem solving in their disciplines. These intuitions cannot be accepted uncritically, but they are probably the best guidelines we have for defining how to proceed with more detailed studies.

With all their strong points, however, these instructional programs in problem solving remain idiosyncratic products of enthusiastic individuals. Although these programs almost certainly do achieve some benefits, it is not clear through what mechanisms these benefits come about. This lack of knowledge leads to the third major difficulty in work on problem solving in the practical classroom. However effective instruction may be locally, it is hard to extend it reliably beyond its initial context, because one doesn't know how it works. It is even hard to preserve a good instructional program when its innovators depart or turn to other interests. If, however, one could begin to understand in useful detail how some of these instructional programs achieve their effects, then this knowledge could be systematically applied by others, or incorporated into the design of materials addressed directly to the student.

To summarize the situation in the practical classroom then, work in this area suffers from three major difficulties: (1) problem solving is intrinsically very hard to teach, and this is particularly true in the areas of mathematics and science; (2) educational research has traditionally not used methodologies productive in providing information about problem-solving processes; and (3) although some individuals have produced instruction that seems to be effective in helping students to solve problems, very little is known about how this instruction works. What is needed, and is not available, is believable research that elucidates the mechanisms of problem solving at a level of detail useful for designing instruction. Current educational work has not really addressed these mechanisms systematically. The best information available consists of the insights of good instructional developers, who often have done considerable informal analysis of the processes required for skillful problem solving in their disciplines.

Turning from the classroom to the psychological laboratory, the last 10 years have seen impressive progress. In particular, these years have brought much more knowledge about the step-by-step processing of information that a person implements as he or she solves a problem.

Much of this work has been based on relatively new research methodologies that differ from those traditional in educational research in the following ways. First, the data used consist of detailed observations of individuals rather than rough measures such as test-score distributions. Second, these observations are used to construct relatively complete models rather than simply to distinguish between two alternative hypotheses. Often these models are computer-implemented, simulation models capable of actually producing some aspects of the behavior they seek to explain.

In fact, important insights into mechanisms of problem solving have come from people working primarily with computers, in particular from people seeking to design computer systems that solve problems in intelligent ways (i.e., through processes that are at least qualitatively similar to the processes used by an intelligent human being).

In order to make progress in understanding detailed mechanisms of problem solving, work in this area has understandably emphasized the study of exceedingly structured, formal problems. Puzzles and games have provided particularly fruitful domains. Thus, while the insights of this research are exceedingly interesting, the simplicity of the problems addressed has been a major limitation for those of us interested in problem solving in the practical classroom. Mechanisms of problem solving applicable to ferrying missionaries and cannibals across hypothetical rivers just seem to have no immediate applicability to solving problems by means of the equation of motion. However, on the basis of knowledge gained in these simple domains, it now seems possible to begin to study problem solving in domains that have more of the richness we associate with real-world problems. Thus, to enhance productive research, it would be useful to find domains that offer more richness and complexity than puzzles or games but that still have more structure and limitations than the domain of real problems encountered in professional or personal life. These criteria are satisfied by the domain of probalems often included in science and mathematics classrooms. Thus it is not surprising, I think, that there is a growing body of basic research using classroom problems as an arena.

Thus, in summary, in science and mathematics classrooms, teaching students how to solve problems is one of the most difficult aspects of instruction. Furthermore, the research methodologies most widely used in education are least effective in elucidating mechanisms of problem solving. Clearly, instruction could benefit from what begins to be known both about the mechanism of problem solving and about how to study these mechanisms.

On the other hand, the same classroom problems in mathematics and science form attractively rich but structured arenas for basic research on problem solving. These problems are sufficiently well defined and organized that there is some hope of making progress, but they are sufficiently rich that one might begin to study the variety of skills that characterize humans' solving of "real" problems. Furthermore, the classroom can be a good source of intuitions about mechanisms of problem solving, and a good setting for testing these ideas.

With this basis for fruitful interaction, what kind of research questions are being addressed? The remainder of this chapter considers in turn four mechanisms for problem solving that have been elucidated in the psychological (or computer-science) laboratory. After briefly commenting on some basic research supporting each mechanism, I turn to current work beginning to explicate the role of this mechanism in problem solving in classroom science and mathematics.

GENERAL STRATEGIES

Perhaps the most intriguing idea in work on problem solving is that there might be very general and very powerful strategies underlying skillful problem solving in a wide variety of contexts. If such strategies exist, they are clearly of first importance, because they would allow one to both understand and teach problem-solving skills in general, instead of repeatedly investigating (or teaching) a wide variety of strategies specific to particular domains. Do such general strategies exist?

There are a few general strategies that appear repeatedly in computer programs for solving problems, and evidence also supports their use in tasks that include solving logic and arithmetic puzzles and some aspects of playing chess (Newell & Simon, 1972). I describe briefly three examples of such general strategies and then explore their possible relevance to problem solving in classroom mathematics and science. First, the strategy of means–ends analysis involves assessing the difference between the current state of knowledge about the problem and the state of knowledge required for the problem's solution. This assessment is then used to select an action that reduces any difference between these two states of knowledge. A second example of a general strategy is a kind of planning. It involves replacing the original problem with an abstracted version in which only certain central features are retained. Then this abstracted problem is solved first, and its solution is used as a guide to solving the original problem. Using goals and subgoals is a third general strategy observed in the solving of simple problems. A currently unattainable goal is replaced by a simpler subgoal. When the subgoal is achieved, the solver returns to pursuing the original goal.

But is there an indication that simple strategies like these are applicable to anything beyond well-defined tasks like puzzles and games? In fact, there begins to be evidence that these strategies do play a role in problem solving in the domains of classroom mathematics and science.

For example, Simon and Simon (1978), studying a novice solving kinematics problems, found that means–ends analysis of the known and desired equations explained quite well the order in which this solver applied various physics principles. She apparently assessed the difference between the equations she had and the equation she knew would be needed to solve the problem. She then used this information about the difference between her current means and the desired end to decide what new equations to generate so as to reduce this difference.

The expert problem solver studied by Simon and Simon did not use means–ends analysis; rather he seemed to translate the problem into a "physical representation," which then cued the application of appropriate principles. He thus could solve the simple problems presented to him without means–ends analysis. Thus it seems possible that means–ends analysis is a very general, but inefficient, problem-solving strategy. People may apply it to problems for which they have no better method. One aspect of developing expertise in a discipline would then be the acquisition of less general, but more efficient, strategies.

As a second example of the use of general strategies, John McDermott and I (Larkin, 1977b; McDermott & Larkin, 1978) are developing a computer-implemented model that simulates the order in which an expert subject applies physics principles in solving mechanics problems. This model makes extensive use of the kind of planning mentioned previously—it first abstracts key features of the problem so as to construct a simplified problem. It then solves this abstracted problem and uses the resulting solution as a guide to solving the original problem.

More specifically, the model solver abstracts certain qualitative features of the problem, perhaps corresponding to the "physical representation" constructed by Simon and Simon's expert subject. Using these qualitative features, the solver tentatively selects a method for solving the problem. It then applies key physics principles from that method to generate qualitative information about the problem—for example, information about the direction an object moves. When sufficient information has been generated to solve the abstracted qualitative problem, the model solver elaborates this qualitative solution by generating corresponding quantitative equations to actually solve the original problem.

Greeno (1976) has developed a model that simulates some aspects of the problem solving of students in high-school geometry. This model uses the general strategy of creating subgoals in the following interesting way. Although the original problem and some of the subgoals are completely well specified (e.g., prove triangle QPM is congruent to triangle RMP), some important subgoals are indefinite (e.g., find congruent pairs of sides or angles in the two triangles). The indefinite subgoals allow the solver to look freely for patterns that are generally useful in proving triangles congruent, without being constrained to look for a particular pattern.

Thus it seems that general strategies originally studied in simple laboratory contexts may well play a role in the problem solving required in the practical classroom. The work I've discussed, in physics and in geometry, begins to elucidate this role. To the extent that such general strategies do play a role in problem solving in physics and other areas, direct teaching of such strategies should clearly be a primary ingredient of good instruction in practical problem solving. General strategies similar to those I've mentioned are, in fact, a main part of several problem-solving courses including those of Hayes (1978), Rubinstein (1974), and Wickelgren (1973).

The preceding comments suggest that there may indeed be some general strategies (i.e., some major features) that are seen in skillful problem solving in a variety of disciplines. However, these strategies cannot be implemented without a considerable amount of domain-specific knowledge. For example, in order to use means–ends analysis, the solver studied by Simon and Simon had to know how to assess the difference between the equations she had and the equations needed to solve the problem. She had to know what kind of algebraic manipulations would reduce observed differences. Finally, she had to know how to apply appropriate physics principles to the problem situation in order to produce useful equations. Even more sophisticated domain-specific knowledge was used by the expert solver I observed planning a solution to physics problems. He had to know what kind of features to abstract in constructing a useful simplified problem. He had to know what kind of operations he could apply to solve abstracted problems and how these were to be elaborated when he returned to construct a full solution.

Thus I now turn from the issue of general, domain-independent strategies towards issues of how domain-specific knowledge is organized and used in skillful problem solving.

LARGE-SCALE FUNCTIONAL UNITS

The first mechanism I address is the use of large-scale functional units stored in memory. These units make available coherently bits of information that are often used together. Further, such units provide a pre-assigned "default" structure. When the structure is used, individual items can be changed, but the bulk of the structure can simply remain as it was stored. What is the evidence for such functional units, and how might they function in the classroom?

Shank and Abelson (1977) model how people understand stories by using a variety of large-scale units, one of the simplest being a "script." A restaurant script, for example, specifies much of the common knowledge about restaurants—that a person entering a restaurant is hungry, has money to pay, sits at a table, reads a menu, etc. If the reader of a story has such a script stored in memory, then a story involving a restaurant is comprehensible even if only a small number of items from the script are mentioned explicitly. After noting a few items that indicate the existence of a restaurant, the reader accesses his restaurant script and assumes that it is part of the story.

In solving problems, it also seems likely that people work with similarly large-scale, preset units. For example, Hinsley, Hayes, and Simon (1977) read to people brief sections of algebra word problems. When read the brief phrase, "A river steamer," people were able to respond with statements like: "It's going to be one of those river things, with upstream, downstream, and still water" or "It is going to be a linear algebra problem of current type" and, later, "or else it's a trig problem—the boat may go across and get swept downstream." Thus, from a tiny element of the problem, "A river steamer," the person responding was able to activate an entire unit describing a particular kind of problem (upstream, downstream, and still water) and probably even a large part of its solution (linear algebra problems of the current type).

In an experiment of mine (Larkin, 1977a), I wanted to assess whether experienced physicists had more large-scale functional units for solving physics problems than did beginning students (even when these students did know the individual physics principles). I asked several "experts" and several "novices" (beginning physics students) to think aloud while solving a set of problems. If experts have more large-scale units that specify how to solve pieces of a problem, then the equations that the expert generates should be clustered in time, each cluster corresponding to the application of one large-scale method. In contrast, if the novices have fewer such large-scale methods, the equations that they generate should be more randomly spaced in time, corresponding to access of principles individually rather than as part of larger-scale methods. Figure 8.1 shows graphs made by analyzing the tape-recorded verbal comment of two experts and one novice, each solving five problems from mechanics. The graphs show the percent of sequential pairs of equations as a function of the time interval Δt separating the two equations in the pair. The dotted curves are the graphs that would occur if the subject had generated equations randomly in time. The error bars indicate one standard error in the observed frequency.

In Fig. 8.1, the novice's graph corresponds to a random distribution of his equations in time, supporting my suggestion that, for him, principles are accessed individually. In contrast, the experts' graphs indicate a large number of equation pairs with very small intervening times which reflects a significant clustering in time of the equations he generated. This clustering supports the idea that the expert does recall and use principles as part of large-scale coherent units.

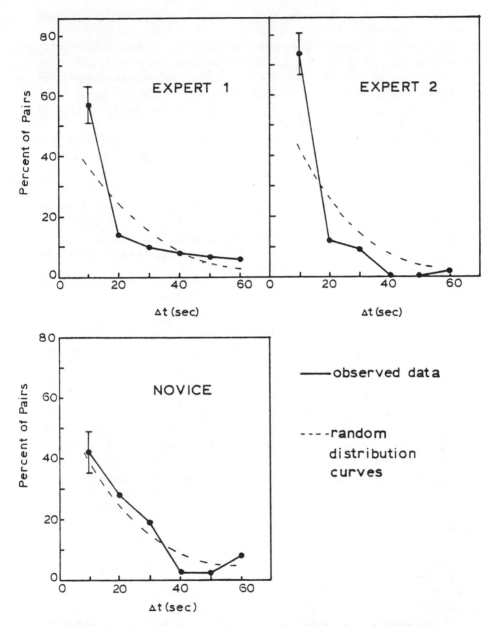

FIG. 8.1. Graphs showing nonrandom clustering in time of equations generated by expert solvers, and random distribution in time of equations generated by a novice solver.

The importance of large-scale functional units is most evident in studies involving domains of practical complexity (e.g., understanding stories, solving physics problems), thus again illustrating the utililty of such domains for basic research in problem solving. This importance of large-scale units also suggests that direct teaching of such units might usefully be incorporated into instruction. One way to do this is suggested by the preliminary work described in the following paragraph, work done by my colleague Fred Reif (with Bat Sheva Eylon) at Berkeley.

They have been investigating the effects of instructional materials that stress a hierarchical organization in contrast to materials that stress a linear sequential organization. In one experiment, two versions of instructional materials presented a derivation of a result in physics. The hierarchical organization, which may have provided students with larger-scale coordinated units of information, enabled students to perform better on a variety of tasks, including: reproducing the derivation, stating the next step of the derivation, finding a "bug" in a similar derivation, and carrying out a similar derivation with a changed premise.

PROCEDURAL KNOWLEDGE

A second major issue in understanding and teaching context-specific knowledge is the distinction between factual knowledge and procedural knowledge. It is not the same thing to be able to state that force equals mass times acceleration, and to be able to apply that principal to generate new information about a problem. How can procedural knowledge be modeled, and what implications might these models have for practical instruction?

In modeling processing for implementing procedures, it is essential to specify not only the actions that can be taken but also the conditions under which each action can be taken. This importance of conditions is made explicit in many computer-implemented models that are written in terms of "productions," units consisting of an action together with a condition specifying when the action is to be taken (Newell, 1973; McDermott, 1978). According to such models, the human mind has stored an immense number of these condition–action units. Whenever the current situation satisfies one of the conditions stored in memory, the corresponding action is implemented. To give a very simple example, when the condition of seeing a red light is satisfied, the action of stopping a car is taken.

More generally, the condition–action unit is a useful way of describing complex psychological processes at a variety of levels of detail. For example, Collins (1976) is working to develop a global theory of socratic tutoring by specifying actions (questions the socratic tutor can ask), each with an associated condition specifying when that kind of question is asked.

In work quite directly relevant to the physics classroom, Klahr and Siegler (1977) have used condition–action units to describe the developing abilities of children to reason about the balance scale. Their work suggests that young children have very simple sets of condition–action units. For example, if there is more weight on the right, then predict it goes down on the right. With increasing experience and age, these condition–action units become more sophisticated and complex. For example, the preceding unit might be modified to: If the distances from the fulcrum are the same, and the weight is larger on the right, then predict it goes down on the right. Older children, who can reliably predict how the beam will tilt, have the most extensive set of condition–action units. For simple conditions (e.g., distance same, weight different), they have simple actions (e.g., predict the heavy side goes down). For more complex conditions, they have more complex actions (e.g., applying the physicists's "torque law"). Interestingly, however, these proficient children do not routinely use the general torque law, even though it would always give correct predictions. I suspect that when an action is complex (like applying the torque law, then it is advantageous to remember also some simpler actions (together with their special conditions). The reason is that these simpler actions are less demanding and less prone to error.

Would it be generally useful to teach directly procedural knowledge relevant to problem solving? In an effort to explore this possibility, Bat Sheva Eylon, working with me at Berkeley, has developed several alternate versions of instructional materials for Archimedes Principle. In one version, students receive a conventional textbook presentation of factual information, together with a few worked examples. In the other two versions, they receive in addition direct instructions in the procedures needed to apply these principles. In one case, these procedures are specified in a sequential list of directions. In the other version, students are encouraged by the organization and activities of the materials to collect these directions into functional units of the procedures likely to be applied together. Preliminary results suggest that neither the factual information alone nor the addition of a sequential list of directions enables students to solve problems very well. However, explicit instruction in functional procedural units substantially facilitates student ability to solve problems.

A second example of directly teaching procedural knowledge is the work of Landa (1974, 1976). His instructional designs in a variety of areas (e.g., Russian grammar, mathematics, problem solving in science) assume that learners can fairly readily learn to execute simple actions. He then focuses on teaching the conditions to guide the selection and use of these actions.

PROBLEM REPRESENTATIONS

The final mechanism of problem solving that I consider is the selection and use of facilitating problem representations. Simon and Hayes (1976) have investigated this issue, using puzzles similar to the well-known Tower of Hanoi. In their studies, a solver's proesses and chances of success depend crucially on whether he represents the problem as the motion of objects or the transformation of objects into other objects.

There is also considerable work on the role of problem representations in the solving of textbook physics problems. Three running artificial intelligence programs that solve mechanics problems all begin by translating the original verbal representation of the problem into some pictorial representation. This pictorial representation then can be used to answer directly certain qualitative questions (de Kleer, 1977). Alternatively, the spatial relations in this representation can serve as a basis for applying physics principles to generate equations (Novak, 1977).

An experiment of mine suggests directly the importance of skillfully using problem reprsentations in physics, particularly qualitative theoretical representations. I asked six persons experienced in physics to solve a difficult problem that could be solved in several ways (some ways easier than others). Of the six individuals, five made reasonable progress; these five constructed one or more qualitative representations that corresponded to various possible theoretical approaches to the problem. For example, they drew force diagrams or listed the sources of virtual works. On the basis of such a qualitative representation, a solver decided whether or not the theoretical approach was feasible, and either discarded it or began to construct corresponding quantitative equations. In no case was the theoretical approach changed after the solver began to construct equations. Thus qualitative theoretical representations would seem to be crucial in the important task of selecting an approach.

In modeling the processes of an expert physicist who is solving mechanics problems, John McDermott and I are working to construct a program that constructs and uses a sequence of problem representations (McDermott & Larkin, 1978). Based on the original verbal statement of the problem, a pictorial representation or "sketch" of the physical situation is constructed. From this "sketch," the model then constructs a qualitative representation of various relevant theoretical objects. For example, it might construct a force diagram or a potential energy curve. The model works extensively with this qualitative theoretical representation, using it to assess whether the corresponding theoretical approach is both appropriate to the problem and feasible to implement. If the approach passes these tests, the model turns to constructing its final representation of the problem, a set of quantitative equations that (if things are working right) can be solved for the answer to the problem.

McDermott and I are also beginning to work on a program that would model the processes of a beginning physics student who is solving mechanics problems. Like the expert program, we are designing it to simulate the order in which principles are applied by human subjects (in this case, beginning students). We think the major difference between the expert and the novice programs will be the use of the qualitative theoretical representation. Preliminary analysis of the problem solutions of beginning students suggests that they translate a problem quite immediately into quantitative equations without making use of the extensive qualitative analysis that forms a large part of the expert's solutions.

All of these comments suggest strongly that constructing good problem representations, particularly qualitative representations, is a very important part of skilled problem solving in physics.

SUMMARY

I've discussed in this chapter what I think is a particularly fruitful interaction between basic psychological research on mechanisms of problem solving and practical classroom efforts to teach effective problem solving. The reasons for this interaction are basically the following. On the one hand, for the study of problem solving, classroom science and mathematics provide arenas that are sufficiently well defined and structured that there is some hope of making progress but that are sufficiently rich that one can begin to study they variety of skills characterizing humans solving of "real" problems. Furthermore, the classroom can be: (1) a good informal source of ideas about mechanisms of problem solving; and (2) a good setting for empirically testing these ideas. On the other hand, in teaching science and mathematics, problem solving is certainly the most difficult aspect. Even good instruction, employing methods based on long tradition and experience, often results in only a few students acquiring a skillful ability to solve problems. Clearly, developers of instruction could benefit from what begins to be known about the psychology of problem solving.

The potential for fruitful interaction between the classroom and the laboratory is illustrated by the research I've reviewed here. This research begins to elucidate mechanisms for solving problems of the kind often encountered in studying mathematics or science. Thus knowledge of these mechanisms can begin to provide some direct guidance for designers of instruction.

REFERENCES

Bauman, R. P. Teaching for cognitive development. *Andover Review: A Journal for Secondary Education,* 1978, *5* (1), 83–100.

Bloom, B., & Broder, L. *Problem solving processes of college students.* Chicago: University of Chicago Press, 1950.

Collins, A. Processes in acquiring knowledge. In R. C. Anderson, R. J. Spiro & W. E. Montague (Eds.), *Schooling and the acquisition of knowledge.* Hillsdale, N.J.: Lawrence Erlbaum Associates, 1976.

de Kleer, J. Multiple representations of knowledge in a mechanics problem solver. *International Joint Conference on Artificial Intelligence,* 1977, *5,* 299–304.

Greeno, J. G. Indefinite goals in well-structured problems. *Psychological Review,* 1976, *83,* 479–491.

Hayes, J. R. *Cognitive psychology: Thinking and creativity.* Homewood, Ill.: The Dorsey Press, 1978.

Hinsley, D. A., Hayes, J. R., & Simon, H. A. *From words to equations: Meaning and representation in algebra word problems.* In M. A. Just & P. A. Carpenter (Eds.), *Cognitive Processes in Comprehension,* Hillsdale, N.J.: Lawrence Erlbaum Associates, 1977.

Klahr, D., & Siegler, R. S. The representation of children's knowledge. In H. Reese & L. P. Lipsitt (Eds.), *Advances in child development.* New York: Academic Press, 1977.

Landa, L. N. *Algorithmization in learning and instruction.* Englewood Cliffs, N.J.: Educational Technology Publications, 1974.

Landa, L. N. *Instructional regulation and control.* Englewood Cliffs, N.J.: Educational Technology Publications, 1976.

Larkin, J. H. *Problem solving in physics* (Tech. Rep.). Berkeley: Group in Science and Mathematics Education, University of California, Berkeley, 1977. (a)

Larkin, J. H. *Skilled problem solving in physics: A hierarchical planning approach* (Tech. Rep.). Berkeley: Group in Science and Mathematics Education, University of California, Berkeley, 1977. (b)

Lochhead, J. Teaching students how to learn. In *Proceedings of the Third International Conference on Improving University Teaching.* College Park: University of Maryland Press, 1978.

McDermott, J. Some strengths of production system architectures. In *NATO A.S.I. Proceedings: Structural/process theories of complex human behavior.* The Netherlands: A. W. Sijthoff, International Publ. Co., 1978.

McDermott, J., & Larkin, J. H. Representating textbook physics problems. In *Proceedings of the 2nd national conference of the Canadian society for computational studies of intelligence.* Toronto: University of Toronto, 1978.

Newell, A. Production systems: Models of control structures. In W. G. Chase (Ed.). *Visual information processing.* New York: Academic Press, 1973.

Newell, A., & Simon, H. A. *Human problem solving.* Englewood Cliffs, N.J.: Prentice-Hall, 1972.

Novak, G. Representations of knowledge in a program for solving physics problems. *International Joint Conference on Artificial Intelligence,* 1977, *5,* 286–291.

Rubinstein, M. F. *Patterns of problem solving.* Englewood Cliffs, N.J.: Prentice-Hall, 1974.

Shank, R., & Abelson, R. *Scripts, plans, goals, and understanding.* Hillsdale, N.J.: Lawrence Erlbaum Associates, 1977.

Simon, H. A., & Hayes, J. R. The understanding process: Problem isomorphs. *Cognitive Psychology,* 1976, *8,* 165–194.

Simon, D. P., & Simon, H. A. Individual differences in solving physics problems. In R. Siegler (Ed.), *Children's thinking: What develops?* Hillsdale, N.J.: Lawrence Erlbaum Associates, 1978.

Woods, D. R. *Survey of ideas for teaching problem solving.* (Tech. Rep.). Hamilton, Canada: Department of Chemical Engineering, McMaster University, 1976.

Whimbey, A., & Whimbey, L. *Intelligence can be taught.* Stamford, Conn.: Innovative Science, 1978.

Wickelgren, W. A. *How to solve problems.* San Francisco: Freeman, 1973.

9 Prescriptive and Descriptive Approaches to Problem Solving

Michael Scriven
University of San Francisco

(1) Everybody working on problem-solving has a favorite typology, and perhaps it's more important here than in more fully developed areas, so I'll begin with mine. The traditional approaches to problem solving have tended to focus on two kinds of problems: (1) mathematical or physical problems of the kind encountered in the classroom, and game problems, which I'll lump together and call *within-paradigm* problems, or problems of the first kind; and (2) problems requiring a radically new approach or paradigm or theory or insight or trick, which I'll call *new-paradigm* problems, or problems of the second kind. Most puzzles and some arrangement problems and concept-learning tasks are of this kind. I want to focus on another type (or types) of problem, which I think involves different cognitive and pedagogical difficulties; I'll lump these together for the moment as problems of the third kind. Problem solving in the humanities may be generally of this third kind, but it's also common in the practical sphere; it may also be appropriate or useful to describe the third kind of problem as nonlinear in a sense (I'll explain in more detail later). Jill Larkin favors a distinction that is close to the one I've described between structured and unstructured problems: But I think there are "new paradigm" problems even within a very structured problem situation such as chess or Master Mind.

(2) Before going on to discuss these types in a little more detail, let me discuss another distinction—not a new one, but one that I think we have to reformulate. This is the distinction between the psychology and the pedagogy of problem solving, which is analogous to the distinction between computer simulation and computer success (artificial intelligence) with respect to a particular cognitive problem. The distinction is familiar enough when

127

phrased in those terms, but there is another and more controversial way to phrase it to which I wish to object. It is often referred to as the difference between the scientific approach and the normative approach; but I want to stress strongly that that way of conceptualizing it is completely fallacious. It is actually the difference between *two* scientific approaches—that of descriptive science and that of normative science. Let's take a particular case. When we are looking at protocols of student approaches to a standard math problem, we try to give the data some structure in summarizing it, we "idealize" it, so to speak; and we can easily idealize it in the direction of *efficiency,* in terms of "the *right* way to do it." I am sure—perhaps it's obvious—that one reason for doing this is the interest in *teaching* problem solving, in *improving the skill,* that is part of the motivational structure for most of us and for this conference. But, from the point of view of scientific model building, that consideration is usually said to be irrelevant—we should, it is said, be more interested in an idealization that generates mistake data just as accurately as solutions, the mistakes made by actual problem solvers. And simulators have in fact worked hard to generate models that do simulate the error patterns rather than exhibiting solution strategies.

But we need to be acutely aware of the parity of scientific merit as between the two approaches. The normative sciences have had a bad press but a great undergound; psychotherapy, pedagogy, welfare economics, penology, game and decision theory, latent function analysis, political theory, policy analysis, program evaluation, have progressed quite nicely even though they have all been heresies according to the received doctrine of value-free social science, sometimes misleadingly called *empiricism.* Much of the contribution of cognitive psychology, especially of problem solving, will be lost if we allow the tyranny of the dust bowl to prohibit the development of normative oases. When we discover blind alleys in the protocols, let us ask *both* how they were generated *and* how they can be avoided. It is a serious error to think that the answer to the first is either necessary or sufficient as a step toward the second. Researchers in problem solving must be consciously schizophrenic with respect to their descriptive and normative tasks as scientists. If they have to make a choice in allocating their research time, let me strongly endorse the need for the normative approach.

Perhaps an analogy would be helpful. In developmental cognitive psychology, one of the most interesting researchers in the Piagetian tradition is Kohlberg, with his six-stage theory of moral development. But, despite the cross-culture confirmation of that account, one must remember that it reflects development in societies whose approach to moral education is so backward as to be absurd, societies with virtually complete taboos on discussion in the schools of morally controversial material, taboos that effectively preclude even the first step of moral education, which is presumably serious discussion of current moral problems and alternative suggested solutions to them. One cannot regard it as appropriate for the psychologist to focus *all* of his or her attention upon the artefacts of a primitive approach, and *none* upon developing better ways to do the job. For example, I think that a crash course in practical ethics can compress most or all of those six stages into a single jumble of a few months and probably produce a huge percentage of "impossible" stageskipping. The search for better ways is just as important in dealing with cognitive problems from the traditional curriculum as in the moral area, and just as legitimate a scientific activity. It is a bad hangover from adulation of the physical sciences to suppose that there is something particularly important about reporting on the way things *are;* in astronomy, of course, there isn't anything you can do about altering the orbits of the planets, so there *is* something sacrosanct about the task of describing them exactly. But even in chemical engineering, the job of describing how refining plants catch fire becomes less important than (or important only to the degree it assists) the job of designing plants to minimize the risk of fire. And in the psychology of learning, development, and problem solving, this is even more true: Prescriptive may be the first priority (based only on prescientific or the simplest systematic observations), descriptive second—and then some more prescriptive based on the descriptive.

I have recently had occasion to run an experiment that involved collecting 6000 scripts from high-school students in California, who were asked to deal with a simple problem in practical logic. It would be a staggering waste of time to try to develop a model that accounts for the resulting mess in any detail—a model for protocols that exhibit extremely erratic competence in handling the task. We should instead turn to the much more important task of trying to improve this performance. We don't need to understand the minute mechanisms that generate the profusion of errors in order to do this—these mechanisms aren't likely to be of interest, just *because* the results are so bad. *Broad* patterns may be helpful in order to suggest ways to improve. The search for models of error production becomes more worthwhile as we come nearer to closing the gap between good performance and actual performance. It is a fatuous search when a dozen plausible strategies for badly needed improvement lie ready to be tested, and a million "random" errors are being made. The fact that *sometimes* the errors contain clues for remedies in no way supports the substitution of the task of finding a model for them, for the task of finding a way to avoid them. Looking for clues for a prescriptive model is not looking for a descriptive one.

There is one interesting complication of the above distinction—namely, that the *prescriptive* norm is often usable and indeed useful as the *descriptive* norm. The very phrase "ideal type"—originally from psychology and common in sociology—reminds us of this. The so-called "laws of thought," which were in fact rules of logic, provides another example of the crass overuse of prescriptive norms as descriptive ones. But this complication does not undermine the importance of the difference between *typical* cases of prescriptive and descriptive taxonomies.

G. G. Simpson invented the brilliant labels that have immortalized the two approaches to taxonomy of those who conserve and those who multiply categories—the "lumpers" and the "splitters." Some deep psychological difference is reflected in that difference, and I think the same is true for the prescriptive/descriptive approaches to science. I'll use the terms *teachers* and *watchers* for the two as convenient but not, I fear, scintillating labels. The interesting twist in cognitive psychology is that the teachers can't resist taking cards in the watchers' game—in fact, many of them believed the hucksters who said it was the only game in town. And, by and large, they've done very well in that game, too. But they've also become a bit confused and often neglect their native talent for teaching.

So there are two possible directions for the scientific student of problem solving to take—descriptive and normative—and two corresponding directions of idealization in reconstructing problem-solving behavior and mentation—the descriptive norm and the prescriptive norm.

(3) This distinction between two directions of idealization correlates weakly with the previous distinction between types of problems in the following way: people focusing on the first type of problem, the within-paradigm type, tend to idealize in the teacher's way even when they strive for the other—they tend to be "solution strategists." They tend to be optimistic, simulators, problem solvers, and reformers; whereas people focusing on the second type of problem tend to be pessimistic, romantic philosophers, reflectors. In the GPS approach, Wickelgren and Scandura are in the first category, as is Polya; their characteristic tools are rubrics and checklists and strategies and algorithms and schemas and heuristics and decision trees. On the other side, the pessimist-romantics—Popper and Koestler, many of the Gestalters, and Dreyfus—tend to stress the eureka approach, where systematic approaches are transcended in a burst of brilliance, usually explicable (if at all) only in terms of some idiosyncratic or traumatic model from life experience. Nothing much follows from the eureka approach for pedagogy and not much for scientific psychology, in the sense that has usually been conceived, though something may follow for humanistic psychology (in Collingwood's sense, not the touchy-feely one); and of course humanistic psychology (or Gestalt psychology) *may* be the best we can do in *some* areas of psychology. If regarded as general accounts, both accounts seriously distort the psychology of problem solving. The first fails to provide much pedagogical help with new-paradigm problems, as the history of the limitations of GPS amply demonstrates. The second fails to give recognition to the enormous mass of problem solving that proceeds by relatively routine procedures—it is reminiscent of the view that computer chess programs

haven't suceeded in simulating human chess playing because they haven't beaten Karpov.

(4) Against that background, what can we say about problem solving of the third kind? Let's take three examples and see if anything emerges from them. The first problem is whether or not to use micrographics for information storage in a particular office environment. The second is the problem of formulating a set of rules governing conflict of interest for university faculty serving as consultants to federal agencies: An associated more specific problem would be the problem of determining whether a particular individual is in conflict if he/she sits on a panel refereeing proposals that include some from his or her own institution. The third is the problem of developing a model of human problem-solving behavior (Version A) *or* a model for teaching problem-solving skills (Version B); and, of course, there are more specific cases under A and B [e.g., modeling the problem-solving behavior of *this* subject (Scriven), working on *this* problem (defining Type 3 problems)].

Of course, the third of these examples *might* call for a new paradigm and hence be a Type 2 problem, but for reasons that I have expounded elsewhere, I am certain that this is not the case. And I take it that it is fairly obvious that these are not, at least not obvious, within-paradigm examples (i.e., Type 1).

This tripartite typology, now that it is laid out, is obviously much simpler-minded—at least, less technically phrased—than a typology like Greeno's, for example. We clearly have one case of his induction of rules in this third category, but we can also get examples of that in either Type 1 or Type 2. Again, someone very concerned with the difference between real-world problems and artificial or special puzzle or game or formal language problems will think of my categories as missing that distinction; but I don't see that distinction as cutting Nature at the joints, because many standard applied math problems are real-world although formal, and many dubious "solutions" are proposed in game contexts (such as the four triangles with six matches "solution").

What is important about problems of the third kind is that they are commonly found and highly significant in the real world, and they can equally well be found in the world of chess (*Should* one castle early? What considerations *should* affect one's decision to castle and how? What *does* affect players' decisions?).

An enthusiast for either algorithms or eureka phenomena will naturally try to squeeze my Type 3 into one of the other categories—and, of course, there are similarities. But the effort to subsume is not only procrustean, it is herculean. Type 3 problems are too idiosyncratic to be well covered by other paradigms, but by no means so idiosyncratic that a single great insight or analogy will handle the problem. On the other hand, the notion of partial solution makes sense here but scarcely with a eureka problem. And so on. Indeed, I think I prefer the idea that Types 1 and 2 are special cases of Type 3, if we have to get into the subsuming business. But it's better not to procrusteanate.

Look at the dimension of coding difficulty or representation. The problem of finding the roots of a quadratic equation has no coding difficulty: It is a formal problem in a formal language. Predicting the range of a projectile involves some coding difficulties—what approximations to use, what weighting of what variable, etc. The problem of assessing the validity of the line of argument in a political editorial in the New York Times has, presumably, very high coding difficulty, because we can't get experts to agree on how to formalize it into languages where its validity is determinable. The difficulty with Type 3 problems is hardly a coding difficulty at all; on the other hand, it's not *irrelevant* to coding in the way that missionaries-and-cannibals solutions, or the eureka recognition of universal gravitation, seem to be.

(5) A useful perspective on Type 3 problems is to see them (or at least these three examples of them) as *evaluation* problems. The first calls for essentially a cost/effectiveness evaluation of a technology. The second calls for the formulation or application of criteria for evaluating moral or legal propriety with respect to a particular kind of situation. The third requires the evaluation of models or theories, and in the particular case, self-evaluation.

One of the reasons why problems of the third kind have been under-discussed in proportion to their importance is, I suspect, that they *are* evaluative and that evaluation has not been thought of as a legitimate type of rational thought, being classified rather with feeling or taste. Since I think evaluation is probably the most important intellectual skill of all, in science and elsewhere, I have a very different perspective and want to argue strongly for evaluation as a problem-solving process that deserves considerable attention.

Evaluation is not *all* there is to Type 3 problems: Invention or creativity is also required, in all three examples but most obviously in the third; perception in the nontechnical sense of skilled or gifted seeing is involved, too. Yet invention is also one *part* of evaluation, an essential part, so the two should not be sharply separated: Perception is in the same situation.

Now, evaluation is also part of all problem solving; although it's the hidden part, it may be like the hidden part of an iceberg. Even to recognize that a problem exists presupposes the capacity for a negative evaluation of the immediate responses. And to recognize a solution when restructuring or algorithm application turns one up is to evaluate a putative solution favorably. Manufacturing without quality control is not manufacturing, it's garbage production; and inventiveness without evaluation is not problem solving, it's free association, Yet we have not looked very hard at this process of evaluating solutions—and still less hard at those problems of the third kind, where the *solution is sometimes itself an evaluation.* (Rubinstein is perhaps most conscious of the role of values in problem solving, but he sees very little of the deeper entanglement.)

Evaluating a proposed coding or representation of a problem in a problem space is another crucial auxiliary involvement of evaluation; so is the evaluation of the representation of the criteria for a satisfactory solution in that space. In many cases, these "supporting" evaluations are very simple. It is an important and general feature of Type 3 problems that the *identification of a solution involves a nontrivial evaluation*. For example, it is very difficult: (1) to say what a good theory of problem solving would be like (or to know if one has one); or (2) to say what a complete set of conflict of interest criteria would look like; or (3) to identify them reliably without explicit criteria. Hence, the problem of developing such a theory has an *extra* dimension of difficulty by comparison with problems like Nim, solving a set of simultaneous equations, or Archimedes' original eureka problem. This absence of prestateable criteria for a solution makes the means–end and discrepancy-reduction methodology of GPS inapplicable or very difficult to apply.

(6) It has been tempting to dismiss or just castigate such problems as underspecified, ill-defined, or ill-structured, but that is as misleading as saying that the absence of a decidable grammar for English means that we cannot reliably identify a grammatical sentence. We can recognize grammatical sentences in most cases, and we can do about as well in identifying good solutions to Type 3 problems. In particular, we can: (1) easily generate and identify quite poor solutions; (2) rather easily rank-order solutions; and (3) induce successively better criteria for successively better solutions from a study of partial solutions and the cases that cause them trouble. Thus there is a bootstrap phenomenon here that is qualitatively unlike most Type 1 and Type 2 cases.

Note why this is *not* like the oft-noted examples of ill-defined goal status, ill-defined initial conditions, and ill-defined transformations. We need to distinguish between three kinds of "well-defined": explicitly defined, implicitly defined, and reliably recognizable. A goal state, for example, is well-defined as long as it can be reliably recognized by someone who meets certain recognizable conditions on ability and experience. (In fact, it can then be "operationally defined" explicitly, using the suitably qualified and trained observer as the reference instrument.) Implicit definition of a goal state is well illustrated by the absolute zero of temperature—not recognizable in one sense (since not attainable) but fully determinable without any correct explicit definition.

Notice also that one does *not* have to be able to produce an instance of a satisfactory solution to a Type 3 problem in order to be able to show (or argue plausibly) that one could identify a solution (cf. Greeno, 1976).

(7) It seems to me that the primary philosophical problems, to take one example of an area in the humanities, are very much like one or other of our Type 3 examples and very unlike Types 1 or 2. And the progress we have made

in understanding philosophical problems due to the work of Wittgenstein and his school seems to me quite illuminating as we look at the problem-solving literature, because the latter still exhibits the same dependence on formalization, the same respect for explicit definition, that characterized pre-*Investigations* philosophy. There are few better examples in intellectual history of the success of the strategy of moving away from a goal in order to achieve it than the move to mere linguistic analysis in order to solve deep philosophical problems. Of course, many of the "movers away" lost interest in moving back and became entranced with the local goals of analyzing ordinary language with greater care that it had ever received before.

At first sight, it appears as if there are great differences between primary philosophical questions (like "Is there a God?", "Do humans have free will?", "Are there absolute standards of ethics or aesthetics?") and our Type 3 questions. But the relevance is easy enough to explain, because one can rephrase the question about theism as "Is the hypothesis of God's existence *well enough* supported/disconfirmed to justify acceptance/rejection (under various combinations of definitions of "God" and "existence")?", which is an evaluation question of the same kind one would have to face in the course of deciding whether a reasonable theory of problem solving exists. Exactly the same problems of deciding when/whether one has a satisfactory theory and adequate definitions arise in both cases. And we now see, perhaps more clearly with these examples, how the *holistic appraisal of all the evidence* (which requires the judgment that it *is* all the significant evidence) is a key element in solving the problem. The difficulty is not just that we can't *state the solution criteria* explicitly, it is also that we can't *synthesize the performance data* easily. This tremendous problem of holistic synthesis is what I had in mind in saying that problems of the third kind tend to defy linear approaches. Array processing, pattern recognition, and configural scoring seem more appropriate procedures. Problems for judges in the appeals court also exhibit this characteristic; they are being asked to reassess a mass of evidence that is not (typically) itself in dispute. The dispute is over whether this particular mass establishes *guilt* or shows that a *contract* was involved or that a *corporation* existed. It is tempting to classify these as cases of ill-defined criteria, but that is incorrect or at best unimportant, like the Korzibskian move in general semantics. The uncertainty here resides in the legitimacy of the move from the initial conditions to the final condition or conclusion (to use language that is currently employed); the legitimization of the integration [synthesis/perception/gestalt, to use other terms for roughly the same process (or event)].

(8) Unfortunately, although it is appropriate to *try* to reduce this intergration to a linear weighting procedure, and although there is much research supporting the superiority of such an approach over judgmental integration for *certain* types of problems, we fail quite badly as we get nearer

to pattern-recognition tasks and further from prediction-from-data tasks. It does not follow from this difficulty for what is in fact the descriptive approach that we are in any difficulty with a prescriptive/pedagogical approach. We can quite easily *train* people to track lions even if we can't *explain* what the cues and configurations are to which they respond. So the limits of simulations are not even hints of limits to recommendations.

Unfortunately, humanists or gestalters who intuit or infer these limits to the linear approach have tended to wildly proclaim the indispensability or superiority of some special human capability that transcends mechanism and materialism. As the Cornell experiments showed decades ago, it is quite easy to get a perceptron to learn to recognize complexes prior to and possibly without ever being able to say exactly what it is that is being recognized. Humans are complex machines, and even simple machines can do more or less than we can explain, expecially when they *break down* (that term provides another example of prescriptive norms serving as descriptive norms).

Type 3 problems are very amenable to training approaches in which a combination of relevant facts and special skill development rapidly upgrades performance. It is very easy to extend such training to handle a type of problem that at first glance appears rather different (e.g., the "interactive diagnosis" problem, "What is the matter with this patient?", where diagnostic tests are allowed, and part of the training is to teach what tests to call for, as well as how to interpret the results). Such interactive diagnosis problems are obviously closely related to the serial rule induction problem with feedbacks so thoroughly studied by Wason and Johnson-Laird, mostly from a descriptive point of view. (There are also interesting analogies and dysanalogies with gaming.)

(9) The prescriptive approach to problem solving aims to tell people how *to* do it; the descriptive tells how people *do* do it. The first has no commitment to success in prediction (of pretraining behavior); the second does. The first has no commitment to explanation; the second does. But the first does have to be able to produce *justifications* for its recommendations; the second, since it produces no recommendations, does not. Take the simple case where a subject is told that a coin is biased so that it will come up heads 2/3 of the time and he/she is given the problem of predicting, trial by trial, which way it will come up in a series of 50 trials. It's obvious what one should do; it's obvious why; it's rapidly obvious that most people don't do it; it's much less obvious why they don't and it's very hard indeed to say either what a particular person will do in general or on a particular trial. This is a problem that is within-paradigm for someone who understands probability, new paradigm for someone who doesn't. It illustrates the relativism of that distinction and also one way in which people improve their problem solving throughout life. Would someone who understood this problem be caught dead in the Monte

Carlo fallacy? Of course they would, often enough—that's a tough transfer of learning for most people. But they can learn to handle the Monte Carlo case, too. What is the limit to training? We'll never know until school curricula begin to take the lessons of this area seriously and try to teach/train students in proven problem-solving strategies that pay off heavily in the areas with maximal impact on the students' life choices. God knows how many gambling addicts and victims of astrology and how much incompetence or poverty we turn out due to nontraining in the more obvious but currently extrcurricular life skills. The data on conditional reasoning is a monstrous example, and the Evans and Wason study is a lonely start on what should be a busy prescriptive trail.

The humanities *embody* some important models of problem solving of the third kind, but since they haven't learned what those models are, or even how to benefit from their transfer to new situations, they have made too little discernible contribution to the education of most people, except in hours spent. But we should not conclude that they cannot make such a contribution. I think the rewards from studying problems of the third kind, particularly as part of prescriptive science, may well be greater than the many we have reaped—though not yet stacked into the granary—from the study of the first two kinds. And *metastudy* of the humanities may contribute greatly to such work.

(10) The overall design error in much of the work on problem solving to date has been the focus on artificial problems (e.g., rule induction from serial pattern prsentation) without any plan for relating this to real-world problems. This is the same pseudo-Galilean approach that kept the learning psychologists in the rat labs for fruitless decades. Galileo had a proof that the results from his experiments in simplified conditions (rolling the ball down the inclined plane) were immediately translatable into answers to the free-fall problem. We have no such proof even at the plausibility level. Studies of the effect of feedback, pretraining, etc. on serial pattern rule induction are *at best* ways to generate suggestions for research on nonartificial problem solving, and I can see no reason not to approach the problems directly.

So this is a plea for restricting ourselves to real problems, not artificial ones, and for moving the focus on real problems toward those of the third kind. The Greeno typology itself is so impregnated with a particular conceptualization of problem solving that it creates a risk of doing research that cannot be made to yield prescriptive solutions for real problems. Such a risk is lessened by using a more phenomenological taxonomy such as the primitive one suggested here.

It might be replied that any progress in understanding a phenomenon inevitably leads to theoretically impregnated classification schemes. One can hardly obtain much insight into process from the Types 1, 2, and 3 taxonomy. The hard question is: How does one measure insight into process? My inclination is to measure it in terms of *prescriptive pay-off:* This is the point of view of the solution seeker, the fixer, the engineer, the teacher. We must ask: How much improvement *in practice* comes from a new conceptualization? Let me suggest an overall research strategy based on this viewpoint, one that is almost the reverse of the usual approach. We begin by identifying a group of problems that are of substantial educational importance *and* can present substantial difficulties to those who have to learn how to solve them. We focus on improving the methodology of instruction by whatever radical or regular means we can find, looking for clues in student protocols, observations of superteachers, the bag of tricks from other areas, etc.—even looking at problem-solving research for ideas like Dr. Groot's discovery about search strategies in master chess players. Then we do the same for another group of problems, its separateness being defined simply by the fact that the students who have been through our first fix have undiminished trouble with the second. Note that we stick with the same students. We are hoping for synergistic effects, and we are counting on serendipitous ones, but we are doing something worthwhile anyway. We run an occasional control group to check for the existence of such effects and track them down when they surface. Simultaneously, we struggle hard to build explanations of our successes—but very low-level explanations whose humble tasks are to help us in working out some more fixes. If we are *very* lucky, our exlanations *might* generalize across two or three groups of problems from the beginning. We do not anticipate much generalization across subject-matter types of between college and middle-school grades, but we watch and hope for a lucky strike. Given the failure to find communality in the problem-solving processes even in the games research, with the super simplified criterion definition characteristic of games, we surely have no options on this last point.

What this approach yields is pure gold but no glory—that is, we produce a great many fixes, great improvements in learning speed, coverage, or depth, but the chances are not great that we will be remembered for our contributions to theory. This approach—the teacher's approach to research as opposed to the researcher's approach to teaching—is well exemplified in much of the SESAME work. I am thinking for example of Mark St. John's recent doctoral dissertation, which involved a successful multiple-thrust approach to upgrading learning in a physics lab course. And I follow this pattern in teaching practical reasoning skills and practical ethics. Of the best-known references, perhaps Wickelgren is closest to this approach, but he focuses half of his effort on puzzles, not "honest problems."

If you look at the dissemination of knowledge in a field with no pretensions to abstract theory, like bass fishing, wood trimming, or sword making, that's the model they follow, and whenever the evaluation process is fully scientific, the results are steady improvement and some nice low-level theories. But in psychology—even educational psychology—we are up against dreams of Galilean glory; and, in that state of mind, who the hell gives footnote references to great teachers? Yet the data shows that the interteacher variance is often much larger than the intermethod or intermaterials variance, where the usual range of widely hyped methods and materials are involved. It seems crazy to me not to mine for gold where it's lying on the ground and to prefer rapping with geologists, but the evil spell of physics has us in its grasp. Fly-fishing is a more fruitful model. Perhaps hi-fidelity speaker design is a fairer one. But not physics.

(11) Precisely the same mathematical madness is to be found in management science, where we always seem forced to choose between the conclusions of theories of no proven value and the biographies of great business leaders. No one seems capable of identifying any middle-level principles of management, though Drucker may be close at times. Still, "management science" is in poor shape. But I draw no invidious conclusions from the fact that Herb Simon has been notoriously active in both areas. Indeed, his direct descent from William of Ockham has made him a powerful force for formulating minimal useful theory in each area, as witness the Necker cube illusion model. It is interesting that Erickson and Jones (1978) attack the program-as-theory approach exactly on the grounds of lack of parsimony; their reason is that too many "local" considerations get built into programs, different ones for different tasks, and this is in tension with the goals of a general theory. It is; they are right on the point, but wrong on the implied conclusion, because a general theory is inappropriate here. In the same way, they are wrong about the nonfalsifiability of theories-as-programs, supposing that it means explicit formulation of all assumptions as axioms. But that is no more a requirement on a program than it is a requirement on a good blacksmith that he be able to tell you the right quench temperature of 01 steel; the requirement is only that he make good blades out of it and that *we* know how to identify those. Programs whose exact assumptions cannot be explicitly formulated will become increasingly common; they will be tailored to fit the phenomena by tailoring their performance, not some labeled axiom. They will become more human *in that* they can be trained but not axiomatized; the Kurzweil universal font OCR is a good example of this from available technology.

(12) What I am advocating is not the abandonment of teaching any kind of heuristic. It is rather the teaching of lower-level heuristics plus their self-application. For example, in teaching product evaluation, I do it by exhibiting checklists, assigning the development of checklists, and finally having the class develop a checklist for developing checklists. In teaching the design of reports, I follow the same sequence, with the final step being an examination of my presentation against a general set of criteria for presentations. We can make a good case for this much generalization. It is

only for a collection of puzzle and program freaks (like us) that one can make much of a case for GPS-type heuristics, or even, I think, means–end analysis.

Interestingly enough, there is a large unexplored territory of the "methodology of modest devices" like checklists, and profiles like the MMPI, or tree diagrams, or ideal types, taxonomies, and successive approximation procedures. They have been largely ignored except by practical people like airline pilots, because they aren't theoretical enough for the Newtonian dreamers or subject-specific enough for textbooks. I think it is the most promising territory ahead for problem-solving research. We might call it the study of heuristics of the middle ground, which correspond for prescriptive science to what are called theories of the middle ground by descriptive scientists.

REFERENCES

Greeno, J. G. Indefinite goals in well-structured problems. *Psychology Review,* 1976, *83,* 479–491.

10 Teaching Problem-Solving Mechanisms

John R. Hayes
Carnegie-Mellon University

INTRODUCTION

Since Larkin is one of the best and clearest minded researchers now working in the topic area of this conference, I am pleased to be able to use her paper as a vehicle about which to weave a discussion of problem-solving courses. Larkin discusses four categories of problem-solving mechanisms: general strategies, large-scale functional units, procedural knowledge, and problem representations. I agree with her that problem-solving courses such as those of Rubinstein (1975), Wickelgren (1974), and myself (Hayes, 1976) emphasize general strategies such as means–ends analysis, planning, and abstraction. However, I add two notes to her observation:

1. *There is more than one kind of problem-solving course.* Alan Schoenfeld (1978) has developed a course restricted to junior- and senior-level math majors that builds on a great deal of domain-specific knowledge. Most of the problem-solving techniques that he teaches are specific to mathematics rather than general. The wide difference between the more special courses and the more general ones was made dramatically clear in a recent incident. Schoenfeld's department head was so enthusiastic about the course that he advertised it for the spring semester and invited freshmen of all persuasions to take it. Schoenfeld is now very actively designing an entirely new course to meet the needs of this less sophisticated audience.

It appears, then, that problem-solving courses may be taught at different levels and that the different levels may emphasize different problem-solving mechanisms—the lower-level courses emphasizing general procedures and the upper-level courses emphasizing domain-specific knowledge. I think that it is greatly to the credit of Richard Teare, David Tuma, and their colleagues to have designed and implemented a three-level problem-solving course years before this conference was convened. The first-level course is designed for freshman and sophomore students in all of the science and engineering departments. As the following course description shows, the course requirements are very general:

39-100   Units each semester 9
Analysis, Synthesis and Evaluation
Analysis, synthesis, and evaluation in the context of realistic engineering situations. The student learns through practice to deal with problems that require the use of skills that include modeling, analyses that range from mathematical to heuristic, the use of experimental methods, inventing, making judgments of value and need, and the making of decisions and recommendations. Problems are chosen to reflect the level of the course and the background of the students. 2 hrs, rec., 2 hrs. tutorial/lab. Prerequisite: Physics I, Calculus I, Chemistry.

The second level consists of five different courses taught to juniors. Each is aimed at a special departmental audience in metalurgy, chemical, civil, electrical, or mechanical engineering. Each course focuses on problem solving within the departmental discipline but uses principles from the other disciplines as well.

At the third level, students from the various disciplines are again united in a single two-semester course:

39-320   Units each semester 12
Analysis, Synthesis and Evaluation IIIa
An interdisciplinary problem-solving project course in which students work as leaders or members of project teams under the guidance of faculty advisors. The projects are chosen from a variety of engineering areas with new problems selected each semester. Oral and written presentations concerning the results of the project studies are required.

39-322   Units each semester 12
Analysis, Synthesis and Evaluation IIIb
A sequence of design problems from a broad range of engineering areas will be considered. Students from several engineering disciplines will work together to reach a sound conclusion using the tools from their previous courses. Oral and written reports on the individual design problems will be required.

Student evaluations show that these courses are very well received.

We should also note that there is a vigorous tradition in the teaching of problem solving that we have not discussed in any detail at this conference. This is the tradition in the visual arts, represented by books such as *The Universal Traveler* (1974), by Koberg (an architect) and Bagnall (a graphic designer), and *Experiences in Visual Thinking* (1972), by McKim (a graphic designer). People working in this tradition seem much more concerned with problems of idea generation and spatial representation than with problems of heuristic search.

2. *A first-level problem-solving course can do more than teach general strategies.*   Again, I agree that many first level courses do emphasize general strategies. Furthermore, I think that it is important that they do so. However, I believe that such courses can and should present information about all four of the problem-solving mechanisms that Larkin has discussed.

To make this discussion concrete, let me describe the problem-solving course that I am now teaching with Lynne Reder. This course is being taught to all freshmen in the College of Humanities and Social Sciences at Carnegie-Mellon as part of the core curriculum. It has no prerequisites and, thus, is even less specialized than the Analysis, Synthesis and Evaluation course described earlier. The objective of the course is to improve problem-solving skills useful to students in the humanities, social sciences, and arts. It is divided into four major sections:

1. Information acquisition (memory and learning)
2. Decision making
3. Problem solving (representation and search)
4. Creativity

In the problem-solving section, we do teach general strategies such as hill climbing, means-ends analysis, and planning, but we teach the other three problem-solving mechanisms as well. Students learn about large-scale functional units such as chunks in the memory section and about schemas and macro-operators in the problem-solving section. They learn about the nature and importance of representations, and they learn specific representations for a number of problem types. Further, in all sections of the course, the students acquire procedural knowledge. In the memory section, students learn to use mnemonic techniques such as the keyword technique and the method of loci. In the decision-making section, they learn to *do* satisficing and additive weighting, and to *apply* Bayes' Theorem in solving problems. In addition, they learn skills such as brainstorming and drawing in two-point perspective. I believe that a general problem-solving course should teach all four problem-solving mechanisms.

EVALUATION

Larkin discussed a number of problem-solving courses that appeared to produce good results for unknown reasons. She suggests that they are "the idiosyncratic product of enthusiastic individuals." If this were the case, such courses would not be exportable to other teachers at other universities. However, one enthusiastic individual at this conference, Rubinstein, claims to have exported his course. He said that Bartlett at St. Louis had found that students participating in a Rubinstein-type course showed a significant increase in IQ as a result. I expose my own prejudices by saying that such a result violates my prior assumptions about the evaluation of problem-solving courses. I would not have expected a course like Rubinstein's to improve the skills measured in IQ tests (e.g., vocabulary, memory span, spatial relations) to any significant degree; rather, I would expect such a course to influence the skills specifically taught (e.g., general problem-solving skills such as means–end analysis and working backward). In short, I simply don't believe the result.

In my own problem-solving course, I have done some evaluation of specific skills taught. Many of the mnemonic techniques are easy to evaluate because their results are so dramatic. In the method of loci, the student is taught to associate items to be learned with locations in a familiar place such as a house or building. Students are expected to be able to use the technique to remember a list of 20 items presented at the rate of 5 seconds per item. Table 10.1 shows the performance of a class of students who had learned this technique.

The keyword method is used to learn foreign language vocabulary. In this technique, the student associates an English word that sounds like the foreign language word with the meaning of the foreign language word. Table 10.2

TABLE 10.1
Distribution of Scores on Method of Loci Test

Number of Correct Items	Number of Persons With That Score
20 out of 20	51
19 out of 20	23
18 out of 20	8
17 out of 20	5
16 out of 20	2
15 and below	3

TABLE 10.2
Distribution of Scores on Hungarian Keyword Test

Number of Correct Items	Number of Persons With That Score
10 out of 10	87
9 out of 10	3
8 out of 10	2
7 out of 10	1
6 or below	0

shows the performance of students using the keyword method to learn Hungarian words at the rate of 30 seconds per word.

Evaluation of decision-making skills is complicated by the fact that decisions depend on individual values. If two people choose to buy different types of cars, it doesn't follow that one of them is wrong or has a faulty decision procedure. It may be that the two have different values. However, if an individual can't agree with himself, that does seem to be reasonable evidence of a faulty decision procedure. It was this sort of evidence that we used to evaluate decision procedures in our students.

Both before and after being taught decision procedures, the students were asked to rank order their choices among several apartments. A typical apartment set is shown in Table 10.3. What the students didn't know was that several of the sets of apartments were identical. By using identical sets, we

TABLE 10.3
Student Apartments

	B1		B2
distance from place of employment:	20 minutes	size of rooms:	spacious
brightness:	fairly bright	cleanliness:	all surfaces need scrubbing
cleanliness:	ready to move in	brightness:	dim
landlord attitude:	very friendly	kitchen:	stove, sink, and refrigerator in good condition
noise level:	sometimes noisy		
kitchen:	stove, sink, and refrigerator old but usable	general repair	needs one day repair work
size of rooms:	comfortable	landlord attitude:	hostile
general repair:	needs 1 week	noise level:	always quiet
		distance from place of employment:	45 minutes

	B3		B4
general repair:	needs no repairs	distance from place of employment:	15 minutes
kitchen:	stove, sink, and refrigerator in good condition	landlord attitude	indifferent
		general repair	needs no repairs
size of rooms:	cramped	room size:	average
cleanliness:	needs vacuuming	noise level:	frequently noisy
landlord attitude:	cordial	kitchen:	new stove, sink, and refrigerator
noise level:	usually quiet		
distance from place of employment:	60 minutes	cleanliness:	needs vacuuming
brightness:	very bright throughout the day	brightness:	always needs artificial lighting

TABLE 10.4
Mean Disagreement Scores

	Before Training	After Training
Mean Disagreement Score	7.32	3.80

Number of Students		
Better After Training	Same Before & After	Worse After Training
49	8	14

were able to determine the extent to which our students agreed with themselves both before and after training in decision techniques. Table 10.4 shows both mean disagreement scores before and after training—a high score means lots of disagreement—and the number of students whose scores got better or worse.

Evaluations such as these show clearly that we can teach specific skills. Although results of this sort are encouraging, they are limited. These evaluations were conducted by the people who taught the course within the walls of the classroom where the skills were learned. Sometimes the classroom walls seem an impenetrable barrier for knowledge. With discouraging frequency, what is learned inside the room cannot be used outside. Simon relates an experience he had when he and another professor were teaching the same group of students in back-to-back courses—one at 10:30 A.M., and the other at 11:30 A.M. Since they were giving their exams on the same day, they thought it would be interesting to exchange them—that is, to give the 10:30 exam at 11:30 and vice versa. Afterall, the students had to have done all their studying for both courses before the first exam, so what trouble could it cause? Well, it could and did cause considerable trouble, consternation, worry, distress, and general yelling and screaming.

Our humanities college has recently instituted a core curriculum program, and some effort is made in each course to identify relations between it and the other courses of the core. A result has been a common complaint among students that sometimes "I can't tell the difference between English, psychology, and philosophy." It is interesting that students should feel the need for clear boundaries between courses—boundaries that may indeed limit the transfer of problem-solving skills from one course to another.

If we are to do evaluation of a problem-solving course well, we have to show that the students spontaneously use the skills we have taught them outside the confines of the classroom in which they were learned.

REFERENCES

Hayes, J. R. It's the thought that counts: New approaches to educational theory. In D. Klahr (Ed.), *Cognition and instruction*. Hillsdale, N. J.: Lawrence Erlbaum Associates, 1976.

Koberg, D., & Bagnall, J. *The univeral traveler*. Los Altos, Calif.: William Kaufmann, 1974.

McKim, R. H. *Experiences in visual thinking*. Monterey, Calif.: Brooks/Cole, 1972.

Rubinstein, M. F. *Patterns of problem solving*. Englewood Cliffs, N. J.: Prentice-Hall, 1975.

Schoenfeld, A. H. *Can heuristics be taught?* Unpublished manuscript, University of California, 1978.

Wickelgren, W. A. *How to solve problems*. San Francisco: Freeman, 1974.

IV

SOCIAL NEEDS FOR PROBLEM SOLVING

11 The Significant Role of Problem Solving in Education

George Kozmetsky
University of Texas

In many respects, higher education has set the pace for problem-solving activities. Several decades ago, education was preoccupied with preparing individuals to solve operational problems. On the other hand, as more complex organizations emerged, greater concern was shown toward the education of persons not only to solve the problems of complex organizations but also to direct and govern these systems. Consequently, a myriad of tools, techniques, and advanced telecommunication devices, equipment, and systems developed from theoretical and applied research.

During the 1960s and 1970s, it became clear that there were strong linkages among institutions that comprise our society that allocate and transform our resources in meeting perceived and real needs. No single entity could function effectively and efficiently without strong interdependences with other organizations within a context of exercising its own independence in an advocacy or adversary position. These linkages delineate an expanded need for decision-making education: that of developing and educating individuals capable of recognizing, structuring, and solving in an orderly way both micro- and macro-level problems.

This newer breed of educated persons is distinguished by the ease with which it moves among industry, government, and educational organizations, and by its ability to tap knowledge and know-how wherever it happens to be. The increasing importance of nonroutine activities require persons who are able to cut across academic disciplines and also capable of interpreting an organization's operations with the longer-range objectives relating to national policy.

The objectives of higher education must include the training of persons who can be managers of technical and intellectual world resources. Among other things, this challenge requires individuals who must: (1) deal with emotional as well as technical changes; (2) converse in the appropriate language of mathematics; (3) communicate with a wide variety of persons from scientists to engineers to accountants to artists; (4) use sophisticated new tools in effective planning and controlling for strategic and tactical decision making; and (5) understand and implement the social and individual value system of our nation.

In short, technological, and social, and cultural changes—individually and collectively—have set up a self-amplifying system in their demands for intellectual resoures. Technology generates new advancements that, in turn, generate still greater need for sophisticated intelligence. The task for education is not merely to select the gifted or excellent student for training but to develop on a broad front all levels of skills to meet the requirements of society. Decision making at the institutional levels requires the newer breed to adapt its ability to learn faster than institutions while maintaining a stable constructive society.

The objective of educational experiences that will serve to prepare the student for active and effctive participation in modern society must be to assimilate the linkages between knowledge as derived from various scholarly fields and *the reality* of problem-solving practices. The educational experience should assist the student in identifying his or her range of information and understanding gained through both academic and practical experience or associations.

PERSONAL CONCEPTUAL CONSTRUCTS

Most students' problem-solving knowledge is derived from academic pursuits—namely, the various fields of study taken in school. Because not all students take the same courses or study the same areas, this means that at all times there will be gaps in an individual student's knowledge. It is safe to predict that each student will face frustration and lack of understanding because of the diversified academic backgrounds found in the peer group. Therefore, the development of problem-solving skills will require both individual and group study. Yet, because of the lack of an epistemology that unifies the piecemeal information acquired under the labels of concepts, techniques, methodology, disciplines, practices, etc., there will be a continuum of overlaps, gaps, and unfortunate frustrations, Each student must, therefore, be encouraged to build his/her own conceptual constructs that will permit the ordering of knowledge into useful problem-solving schema.

An underlying thesis in this analysis is that there is no dichotomy between academic and practical problem-solving strategies when both are used to build a personal set of conceptual constructs. Rather, it is noted that a significant interaction between the "academic" and the "practical" occurs when an individual attempts to build a unified body of knowledge on which to base personal action in the face of problem situations. Jean Piaget (1971) describes the phenomenon as follows:

> If all knowledge at all levels is linked to action, the part played by assimilation becomes clear. Actions are not, in fact, haphazard occurrences, but repeat themselves whenever similar situations arise. To put it more precisely, they reproduce themselves exactly if there is the same interest in a similar situation, but they are differentiated or else form a new combination if the need or the situation alters. We shall apply the term "action schemata" to whatever, as an action, can thus be transposed, generalized, or differentiated from one situation to another; in other words, whatever there is in common between various repetitions or superpositions of the same action.... In the same way, "order schemata" will be recognized in widely differing kinds of behavior, such as making use of certain means "before" achieving a goal, arranging bricks in order of size, constructing a mathematical series, and so forth. Other action schemata are much less general, and their completion does not involve such abstract interiorized operations.... To say that all knowledge presupposes some assimilation and that it consists in conferring meanings amounts, in the final analysis, to the affirmation that to know an object implies incorporating it into action schemata, and this is true from elementary sensorimotor behavior right up to the higher logicomathematical operations [pp. 7–8].

If students are to develop well-ordered action schema, there must be well-designed opportunities for them to integrate their various experiences. This is best done in a problem-oriented setting where the student can test his or her conceptual framework against the complex structure of difficult problems. The setting must be dynamic and must demand the application of a broad variety of strategies for problem solutions to emerge.

The identification of academic and practical problem-solving techniques cannot be found in any set of courses or in any single discipline. The reason for this is that the dynamic nature of both problems and solution strategies leads to continuous change. Some of these changes are expressed in academic and professional specialization journals and publications. Others are incorporated in practice and never reported. This process of problem-solving techniques changes has been referred to as the "knowledge explosion." Most persons know that to date the information technology has greatly amplified the impacts of the knowledge explosion on one's ability to keep current. Therefore, each person has to be selective and identify carefully what knowledge is available to assist in the skillful and effective structuring and solving of a particular set of problems.

INSTITUTIONAL CONCEPTUAL CONSTRUCTS

When an individual applies personal problem-solving constructs to the problems of a particular institution's needs, it is necessary to develop an institutional conceptual construct that will provide the parameters for problem solving.

Institutions for the purposes of developing their conceptual constructs can be viewed as any group that consciously exercises the promotion of a cause. Problem solving for institutions can be viewed as the power to make and execute policy. For purposes of development, and institutional conceptual construct policy can be viewed as the generation of alternatives for action, their method of selection from the alternatives, and, in light of internal and external environmental conditions, a guide to determine present and future decisions.

The parameters of an institutional conceptual construct are:

1. Organization
2. Cause or goals
3. Course of action
4. Operations.

Students need to be assisted in developing a set of personal problem-solving constructs that will enable them to operate effectively within an institutional conceptual construct. This includes the ability to plan, operate, and control the institutions' activities in a coherent fashion. It also includes the ability to identify and develop strategies for meeting the economic, social, and legal responsibilities of the institution.

At this point, there is need to call attention to some of the more emerging issues that link economic responsibilities and social responsibilities. The academic literature treats this by disciplines, and at present it has yet to come up with a generally acceptable framework. However, it is clear that today's problem solvers must be aware that they are responsible for the allocation of scarce resources over and beyond the traditional allocation between natural and human resources. Technology and innovation, both of which are now viewed as a master resource, must be considered in meeting institutional causes as well as national needs in terms of full employment, quality of life, and balance of trade.

Goals and constraints of institutional behavior are directly relatable to the style of problem solving that dominates the institution. Three different styles are recognizable: (1) professional; (2) enterpreneurial; and (3) adaptive.

1. *The Professional Style.* The professional style is characterized, in part, by an emphasis on factors internal to the institution. If an institution is to

grow, the professional style is biased toward basing this growth on opportunities found within the current product/service/market scope. Growth is achieved, then, by more of the same or similar activities. The organization structure most conducive to the professional mode is the centralized hierarchy. This structure gives the best internal picture of the organization and is well suited to an emphasis on control of operations. The time horizon implied by the professional style of problem solving tends towards the short run. This complements both the emphasis on growth internally and on control.

In the private sectors, the professional style is further characterized by the use of return on investment as the prime criterion for selection among alternatives, and by the use of profit as the measure of success. To finance growth, the capital sources selected are usually the traditional ones: investment bankers, private placements, market placements, etc. Firms dominated by professional-style problem solving tend to emphasize domestic production and markets with foreign operations limited to marketing. The limiting factor on the exercise of the professional mode of problem solving has been antitrust.

2. *The Entrepreneurial Style.* Institutional factors limiting growth from within lead to a style of problem solving that focuses on the immediate external environment as a source of growth. The entrepreneurial style emphasizes planning over control. As a consequence, a decentralized hierarchy is the preferred form of organization. This has the effect of decentralizing control into the hands of subordinate managers operating in the professional mode and retains planning as the primary top-management function. The entrepreneurial style operates within a medium-range time horizon. In this style of problem solving, in the private sector, the key measure for selection among alternatives is expected earnings per share, and the criterion of success is growth in earnings per share and price per share. For the entrepreneurial style, growth is financed through the same traditional sources used in the professional style and through private institutional sources (e.g., venture capitalists) as well as by financial leverage obtained in mergers and acquisitions. Firms dominated by the entrepreneurial style tend to engage in international operations in both production and marketing but with a strong national base. Liquidity represents the prime limiting factor on the entrepreneurial style.

3. *The Adaptive Style.* Pushed by liquidity problems and sheer bigness in the private sector and by world-resource scarcities in the public sector, the early 1970s has seen the emergence to a dominant position of a new problem-solving style. What we shall call the "adaptive style" of problem solving has become influential but not in all institutions. In the case of this style, we are for the most part referring only to corporations like fortune 500 or the leading federal and state agencies in the public sector. And even in these institutions,

when we speak of the adaptive style, we are referring to the behavior of only the top management. The adaptive style of problem solving is systems oriented; that is, it involves both internal and external factors on an interinstitutional business, government, education, etc., basis. Emphasis is on design (or adaptive planning) of total systems. Organizational structures are perceived as being fluid and nonhierarchical. Authority and responsibility are results of superior information and not of prestructured relationships. The time horizon on the adaptive mode is the long run. Private exercise of the adaptive style emphasizes asset (human, physical, and technological) position rather than earnings per share or return on investment. Profitability is the measure of success. By profitability is meant: (1) profits that are derived by a firm plus (2) the measure of benefits that are derived from a company's effort by society beyond the company's profits. Capital sources are broadened to include on a global basis both private and public sources such as pension funds and joint business/education/government ventures for financial capital, foreign and domestic educational and governmental organizations for human resources, and international interest institutions for technology. Concerns dominated by the adaptive approach are likely to be true multinational corporations.

Problem solving in dynamic institutions requires a mix of planning activities. There are five levels of planning, each of which has a unique planning concept, time horizon, and central planning problem. The most simple and first level of planning is *operational planning,* which requires short-range goals and a 1–5-year time horizon. The central planning problem to be solved on operational planning is knowing "to do" an activity or set of activities. The second level of planning is referred to as *tactical planning,* which requires a set of medium-range goals and a 5–10-year time horizon. The central planning problem in tactical planning is knowing "how to." In the third level of planning, *strategic planning,* the problem solver must call upon a set of long-range goals, a 10–50-year time horizon, and knowledge of "where" to go with the institution. A fourth and more broad level of planning is *national policy planning,* which involves national goals, such as energy goals, and a 50–100-year time horizon. This level of planning seeks to answer the question of "what to do." A fifth and final level of planning is called *attitudinal planning,* which requires societal manipulation, such as the institution of democracy, and a 100–200-year time horizon. Attitudinal planning requires a knowledge of "why" as it attempts to develop and shape attitudes.

The integration of a problem-solving conceptual framework and an institutional conceptual construct will result in a process of action as follows:

1. *Problem Formulating*—techniques that perceive and formulate those problems facing society and their impacts on institutions.

2. *Model Building*—Relates the formulated problems into a unified usable conceptual model that starts with the current structure and identifies the desired structure over several time periods (e.g., operational, tactical, and strategic planning horizons).
3. *Problem Solving*—Translating formulated problem into understandable opportunities for execution and implementation by all levels of institutional management.
4. *Assessing*—Means for problem solvers to validate the acceptability and efficiency of their solutions, including their ability to make the deficiencies of the formulation, conceptual models, and solution known to the problem formulators.

The complexity of local, national, and international societal problems is overpowering if we maintain traditional approaches to the training and education of our students. No longer can one simply acquire a kit of problem-solving tools and expect to find an appropriate match for any given situation; rather, students must develop personal problem-solving constructs that will enable them to respond in an adaptive fashion to complex situations. The importance of the problem setting to the effective resolution of critical issues suggests that the student must also learn how to develop an institutional conceptual contruct. These are necessary if the problem solver is to be able to marshal the required resources to implement a given course of action.

Higher education has a societal responsibility to bring its resource systems to bear on the problem of developing and implementing educational experiences that will assist students in their task of inventing new strategies for managing new societal concerns.

REFERENCES

Piaget, J. *Biology and Knowledge*. Chicago: The University of Chicago Press, 1971.

V RECAPITULATION

12 Recapitulation From The Viewpoint of a Teacher

B. Richard Teare, Jr.
Carnegie-Mellon University

The stated goals of the Conference "are practical: to encourage the teaching of generally useful problem-solving skills and to provide the know-how whereby such teaching can effectively be achieved." Moreover, the Conference has been organized to promote an "interplay between basic questions and the more applied concerns," to consider what Larkin calls a fruitful interaction between psychological research in the mechanisms of problem solving and the effective teaching of problem solving in the classroom.

My part of the recapitulation is offered from the point of view of a teacher of problem solving in engineering and is directed to the question: What did the Conference provide to make the teacher more effective. Some of the discussion will be illustrated by an example from my own experience.

To me this has been a most interesting meeting because years ago I sought help from researchers in the field of educational psychology, which I thought should be related to the art of teaching in the same way that physical science and mathematics are related quantitatively to the art of engineering. However, not much help was forthcoming, at least not as much as one might wish, and this is confirmed by later statements of Larkin. Even now there seems to be no methodology of problem solving of wide generality. For example, Greeno said that an analysis that he made led him to conclude that there is no single homogeneous set of skills that can be identified as the important skills of problem solving. However, in the absence of such a set, some good heuristics have been developed such as those that Cyert quoted from Rubinstein's (1975) book, and these are useful to the teacher.

NEED

Let me begin by illustrating the need for the teaching of problem solving to persons who prepare for the practice of engineering. Such a need was felt at the General Electric Company, where, it was said, the engineering graduates that came to the company were good in many ways, notably in doing what they had been specifically taught to do along conventional lines. But many were deficient in dealing with new problems, even the problems that could be dealt with by the use of basic principles that they had learned but that they had applied only in quite narrow and traditional situations—the kind of problems thast Scriven called "within-paradigm". They were lacking in skill at handling his "new-paradigm" problems and his problems of the "third kind." This is an example of what was noted by Cyert: that "many students do not acquire problem-solving skills at an adequate level in college courses through the usual lectures, discussion sections, tests, and problem sets." In the absence of appropriate instruction, many engineers have to acquire necessary and important skills by the relatively unorganized and less efficient procedures of apprenticeship and experience.

Accordingly, more than 50 years ago, the General Electric Company established an in-house educational program, on a part-time basis, running for 3 years, which emphasized the solution of new problems, often ones of current interest within the company, especially in the area of equipment design. When I first became acquainted with the course, admission was limited to 35 graduates, some of whom had master's degrees and, occasionally, a doctorate, The course was considered so worthwhile that graduates were hired for it even during the great depression of the 1930s when recruiting otherwise fell to very low levels. Moreover, the course is still thriving and has been expanded tenfold. Other companies have in-house courses that, like the one at General Electric, emphasize problem solving. It is an interesting fact that, in industry's eyes, education is still lacking in helping students to learn problem-solving skills; we teachers are reminded that our professional schools have not yet caught up with the needs of the real world.

SCRIVEN'S TYPOLOGY

It is helpful to the teacher to think of engineering problems in terms of Scriven's three categories "within-paradigm," "new-paradigm," and the "third kind," although all of these are likely to appear in a single new and challenging problem. Scriven's typology is useful to the teacher in considering what problems he will include in his course. As Scriven points out, the distinction between the first two categories depends on the problem solver—that is, on the extent of his knowledge and experience. Problems that are exclusively within-paradigm tend to be routine and are dealt with in textbooks and handbooks; solving such problems contributes little to an engineer's professional reputation. In fact, engineering technicians are often used on "within-paradigm" problems; their work corresponds to that of paramedics in another field. On the other hand, the solutions to engineering problems of the second and third kind may well be important enough to establish professional reputations (e.g., current problems such as how best to utilize fossil fuel as an energy source, or solar power, or how to store energy economically). More and more problems in engineering involve economic, social, and human factors as well as the basic and engineering sciences; they are of the third kind; and this is the reason for the component of the humanities and social sciences in the engineering curriculum.

Speed in solving problems may well be overemphasized in teaching, especially in problems of Scriven's second and third kinds. This is not to say that time should be wasted but rather that the validity and applicability of the solution and the quality of the resulting design or recommendation are more important than speed.

DESIGNING CURRICULA AND COURSES

Cyert noted the difficulties that face the teacher in defining curricula and courses in professional education. These include choices between specificity and generality, and depth versus broad coverage. It is generally agreed that learning should be directed toward problem solving, but there is no widely accepted plan for teaching general problem-solving skills. There are some artificial problems that give the student an opportunity to exercise some of the techniques he/she has learned, and there are cases that give simulated experience. However, the actual process of functioning as a professional is not well taught in the classroom by these methods. Cyert suggests that to improve education it would be desirable to have a well-developed methodology of problem-solving behavior that would be general and useful in all disciplines and that could be learned by a student as a preparation for learning the specific methods of his/her chosen profession. Rubinstein described a course which is directed to this end. Experiments were conducted by Reif and his group to determine whether students who have had a general problem-solving approach learn to solve problems in a specified field, such as physics or engineering, faster than other students. However, none of the experiments conclusively shows transferability in general.

There is, however, a basis for optimism. Experimental research that started a decade ago is throwing light on human problem-solving behavior and providing a basis for a theory that may well give the help the teacher needs.

Simon discusses the question of generality versus specificity. If basic broadly transferable knowledge and skills are learnable and teachable, there is less need to cover specific topics; If such transfer is limited, as appears likely, although evidence is mixed, we have to deal with specific topics, which means that we have to predict which ones will be important in the graduate's professional life (of some 40 years) in a rapidly changing world—a most difficult task. In the last 40 years, the change in specific knowledge that is useful to engineers has been tremendous, although the core of basic general principles has not changed very much. The conclusion follows that the best teaching strategy is to emphasize principles and methods at the expense of some facts. Moreover, if the education is to be effective, students must learn to apply the principles and to do this not only in existing situations but in new and unfamiliar ones. In this way, we can avoid some of the inefficiency that results from teaching specific facts that have short half-lives.

KNOWLEDGE AND PROBLEM-SOLVING SKILLS

Greeno, Simon, Larkin, and others emphasize the role of knowledge in problem solving and conclude that all problem solving is based upon knowledge; that there is no such thing as expertness without extensive and accessible knowledge; the more extensive, the better. Simon observes that transfer of knowledge and skills from Task A to Task B requires that some of the processes or knowledge used in Task B be the same as some of those used in Task A, an observation that seems eminently reasonable to a teacher. Larkin reported on experiments comparing problem solving of experienced physicists with that of beginning students. Her results showed that the former, who have more large-scale functional units of knowledge and skills at their command (more of Simon's "chunks" of knowledge), could generate clusters of equations in a shorter time and could presumably solve problems beyond the ability of the beginners.

I think this is what Greeno meant by the blurring distinction between "merely applying an algorithm" and "real problem solving", that is, an extensive and accessible knowledge base tends to shift a problem from the latter to the former category.

What was not emphasized as much as it might have been in the Conference was the reciprocal relation—that solving challenging problems extends knowledge and skills and makes them more accessible. To enhance this contribution, the solver should look over the solution he/she has obtained to see what he/she has learned and what has been used that may help to solve future problems. This process also increases interest and motivation through providing a sense of accomplishment.

Simon, and also Larkin, pointed to the distinction between factual and procedural knowledge—that often students have knowledge of principles and facts but have not learned when and how to apply them. Learning may be improved if a student understands and recognizes this distinction.

PRODUCTION SYSTEMS

Simon discussed problem solving in terms of "production systems" or condition–action pairs, which are not facts alone but facts and processes. "A skilled physician recognizes symptoms that evoke possible courses of treatment." Similarly, a skilled engineer recognizes symptoms when his design does not perform as it should, and these guide him in corrective measures.

Simon views long-term memory as a large indexed and cross-referenced encyclopedia. The index enables the problem solver, upon recognizing critical features of the problem situation, to evoke relevant knowledge and possible action. Such pairing is not unlike Larkin's large-scale functional units. Simon mentioned that production systems can be extended by adding new productions.

Production systems have been programmed into artificial intelligence systems, and Simon gives examples. The more information in the problem-solver's long-term memory, the more powerful he/she is as a professional person, such as a physician, scientist, engineer or manager. Recognition of the role of the production system should be helpful to the student in learning to solve problems and hence of value to the teacher.

The production system would seem to apply most directly to problems that are "within-paradigm" in Scriven's usage of the term. The system identifies a paradigm and points to an action. However many, perhaps most, of the "new-paradigm" problems are reduced by creative thinking to a combination of "within-paradigm" components.

Production systems provide models of how learning can take place by self-instruction and by teaching. The latter is not necessarily better because the words of the teacher cannot be stored directly as a production in the student's mind, which Simon called "the fallacy of rote memorization." There must be a conversion of the external words into the internal language of the student's production system; the conversion program must be provided by the learner.

Simon also says that self-instruction need be no more difficult and no different in kind from learning with the help of a teacher by notes that the textbook for self-instruction cannot monitor the performance of the students, observe difficulties, and modify the instruction accordingly. Some of this is done with programmed study texts, and, and with some improvement, by a few automated tutorial programs.

The work reported by Goldstein, which is still in progress, holds great promise for teaching. He advances the methods of computer-aided instruction by adding individualized computer coaching. This goes beyond presentations based on keyword responses to preprogrammed questions to advise learners in a constantly changing context. The coaching function is designed to intervene in student-generated situations to insert a discussion of appropriate skills that might improve the student's performance. For the teacher, this research may be expected to discover more about the learning and teaching of problem solving and how to improve them. It is leading to an improved form of computer-aided instruction and may in addition provide computers that will be of increasing use to human problem solvers.

LEARNING

In science and engineering, the student learns by studying worked-out problems in the text and solving problems at the end of the chapter. Working problems is the most critical part of the learning process, and Simon gives as an example learning how to solve a linear algebraic equation. However, to his text and end-of-chapter problems must be added, possibly in a separate problem-solving course, problems that are not based upon a text. These new problems are needed because of very challenging part of real—problem solving and its associated learning is choosing an approach and devising a plan of procedure; end-of-chapter problems usually are solved by using the methods of the chapter, and the student thereby loses an opportunity for practice in planning.

The role of the teacher is to provide the student with an appropriate program—whether organized as a production system or otherwise—that a student can then internalize. These are Simon's words; I would interpret for my purposes an appropriate program as being an appropriate problem, or collection of problems, at least in many cases.

The teacher should remember that students learn to solve problems by actually solving them; Simon noted that a person does not learn to ride a bicycle by having the theory explained but rather, mostly, by riding a bicycle. As in learning other skills, in problem solving coaching makes for better results as well as improved efficiency. As a former colleague of mine used to say, "Practice does not necessarily make perfect; in fact, practice without coaching may merely perpetuate mistakes." An important corollary is that we should do more than teach skills; students should learn how to learn new skills and methods.

The question may arise: Where does the teacher find suitable problems for a professional-problem-solving course. Some good sources are papers in professional journals and reports, and the teacher's own experience, together with his/her imagination. Answers and results are best given to the students only after they have their own solutions and in a full discussion of the problem that emphasizes method.

The level of the problem used for learning is extremely important. The problems should, of course, be challenging. Many should be characterized by "new-paradigm" and some should be of the "third kind." If problems are too easy, there is little learning, and if they are so hard that the student gives up, equally there is little learning. The level of difficulty depends on the expertise of the student, just as the classifications "within-paradigm" depend on whether the paradigm is familiar. Similarly, the classifications "structured" and "unstructured" are relative to the problem solver.

EXAMPLE

Let me give an example (taken from Ver Planck & Teare (1954), of an engineering problem that is challenging at freshmen/sophomore level and that will illustrate the use of heuristics and other topics that have been discussed at this Conference:

> You as an engineer are faced with the task of analyzing a form of accelerometer that an inventor has proposed for use in an automobile. You are to recommend to your company whether or not to buy the idea for further development, manufacture, and distribution. The inventor has submitted a crude model, illustrated in Fig. 12.1, to demonstrate his idea. The device is a glass tube bent into a rectangular U shape and containing colored water. It is to be mounted in the automobile with the lower part of the tube fore and aft and the sides vertical. The inventor says that, if the car moves constant velocity, the liquid in each of the two vertical arms has the same height; if the car is accelerating, the liquid

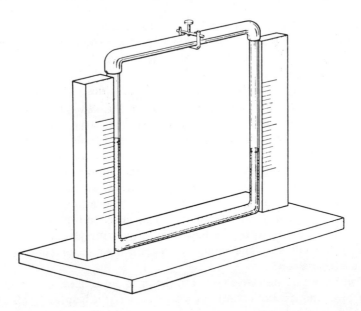

FIG. 12.1.

rises in one arm and falls in the other; if the brakes are applied and the car decelerates, there is again a difference of levels but the direction of the change is reversed. He says that the change of level in one vertical tube as read against a scale gives the amount of acceleration or deceleration. Thus the proposed instrument should be useful in testing the ability of a vehicle to accelerate or the capacity of its brakes to stop it. There is a rubber connection across the top of the U with a clamp, to impede the air flow when the levels are changing. This is for the purpose of damping out the oscillations that occur when the acceleration changes suddenly and that inferfere with the reading of the instrument. The inventor (mistakenly) believes that making the bottom horizontal tube larger than the vertical ones makes the instrument more sensitive—that is, gives a greater change of level for a given acceleration.

We will suppose that you have neither seen nor heard of such a device before, but, in the basic science and engineering courses of your training, you have studied principles that you are confident will be useful in dealing with the problem.

In this problem, the solver is asked whether his company should buy the idea and, if so, how the crude model can be improved. The characteristics of the problem that are of interest in discussing problem solving include the fact that the structure is unfamiliar to most people, that no dimensions are given, that there is more than one way to deal with the structured problem, and that more than one answer may be possible. The solution is not a number but a recommendation. (Information that is not given to the student until he/she has made his/her own study are the facts that this has been invented independently a number of times, has been described in papers, has been manufactured by at least two companies, and is now on the market but probably little used because of its sensitivity to level or tilt, which changes when a car accelerates or decelerates.)

The problem may be dealt with in terms of heuristics such as those Cyert quoted from Rubinstein's book (1975). A good beginning (Heuristic #1 in Cyert's list) is to become familiar with the total picture by going over the elements several times avoiding becoming lost in the details, and (#3) to verbalize by writing out the problem statement. It is preferable for the teacher to assign such a problem orally, the way most real engineering problems are given, so that the student gets practice in Heuristics #1 and #3. The goal of the problem is a recommendation, as in one of Scriven's examples of problems of the third kind. It seems desirable, as Larkin suggests, to first work a simpler problem. This is obtained by asking the right question (Heuristic #5) or at least an appropriate one. This might be: What is the relation between liquid level and acceleration?

Now we have a quantitative goal, but the problem is "new-paradigm" for many people, and it is not obvious how to proceed. It is helpful to talk about the problem, to think out loud heuristic (#10), and to put thoughts in writing as follows.

Consider the horizontal portion of the liquid when the car is accelerating. If there were no net force on it, the liquid would have no acceleration (relative to the earth), and the car would move away from the liquid, which then would back up into the rear vertical tube. Evidently, this creates a greater pressure at the rear end of the tube, which now provides an unbalanced force to accelerate the liquid until it has the same acceleration as the car. We want to find out the relation between the unbalanced force and the acceleration of the car. We search for a principle to apply and think of Newton's law $\Sigma f = ma$. Perhaps for many solvers this may be a production system. The problem is complicated by the fact that the base of the U may not be horizontal and the acceleration may not be constant, and even if it is, the liquid levels will be changing just after the acceleration is applied. So we simplify the model by assuming that the base is horizontal, that the acceleration is constant, and that the liquid has reached new levels that are not changing. This is a second use of Larkin's strategy of replacing the original problem with an abstracted version which is solved first. Thus the engineer seems to have found a principle that may be used, a very simple one, and has started a plan. There still is the question of what mass to use in the equation, the mass of the whole instrument, or of the liquid, or of the liquid in the horizontal part of the tube, or some other mass. Tentatively we will try to work with the mass of the liquid in the horizontal portion. Other questions arise: Does $\Sigma f = ma$ hold for a liquid, and is it necessary to take account of the viscosity of the liquid? After these questions are answered by going back to a physics text or a handbook (the answers turn out to be yes and no, respectively), pictures are drawn (Heuristic #3, also noted by Larkin and others) showing the forces on the mass in the horizontal tube. In this case, the sketch is the free-body diagram that has been emphasized in mechanics books and courses for many decades but resisted by many students. These are the planning and representation steps that were discussed by Greeno.

Next is the execution of the plan beginning with a formulation, preferably in English, of what the principle $\Sigma f = ma$ says about the accelerometer system, identifying forces, mass and acceleration. This is not a general statement of the principle but its application. The statement is then transformed into mathematical symbols. Use of means–end and search procedures involving the expression of forces in terms of pressures and pressures in terms of the heights of the columns leads to transformation of the equation into a useful result—namely, that the difference of levels in the instrument is indeed proportional to acceleration, subject to the restrictive simplifications that were imposed. This part of the solution exemplifies the critical role of means–end and search procedures in a complex problem, which Reif observed in his discussion.

Now, or even earlier, the solution should be checked: by units, limiting values, and any other way that can be devised. In my experience, students hate to spend time checking, yet from the point of view of the practicing engineer, this is as important a step as any. Nor, as Larkin comments, do many students make use of qualitative solutions before translating a problem into a quantitative equation.

Then after the check, one has to think about the effect of the restrictive simplifications, and this leads to additional and more complicated problems. Such is often the case in engineering; for every problem solved, a few more are generated, but fortunately in many cases the new problems are not as critical to the success of the project. Here it turns out that acceleration must be constant, and, as in the case of many instruments, a reading cannot be made until the transient is essentially over. Also, the base must be horizontal.

Solving the problem proceeds by stages: (1) define the problem and devise a goal; (2) plan an attack by choosing a principle, planning how it will be used, and making simplifying assumptions (Stage 2 is only tentative); (3) execute the plan (if it will execute; otherwise modify the plan); (4) check thoroughly; and (5) look into the effect of the assumptions, draw conclusions, and, what is very important, see what has been learned that may be useful in other problems. (These stages are essentially the procedure given by Polya (1952) for solving problems, although this particular sequence was originated independently by various colleagues of mine.)

Here we have learned (by going to references) that Newton's law $\Sigma f = ma$ holds for liquids as well as solids (a being the acceleration of the center of mass of the liquid in the horizontal part of the tube) and that, if the liquid is stationary with respect to the tube as it is in the steady state, there are no viscous forces and no friction force on the liquid.

The engineering problem is not yet finished. Questions arise: How could the given cumbersome model be redesigned for readability, economy, aesthetics, and for simple mounting? Would sensitivity be increased by using mercury instead of water, or water above mercury, or by enlarging the horizontal tube to increase the mass of the liquid in it or in some other way? More problems again. The design can be improved, but the details are probably not germane to this recapitulation.

Finally, there is the question of whether the idea is worth buying and embodying in a manufactured product, which is an example of Scriven's problem of the "third kind." The fact that the devices have been manufactured and sold means that there have been "yes" answers in fact; yet one published paper votes "no" because of the difficulty of keeping the bottom tube horizontal when a vehicle is accelerating or decelerating.

TEACHING

I have outlined the solution to the accelerometer problem in some detail because it provides an example, from an engineering point of view, of so much of what was discussed in the Conference. This problem has been used in a course to illustrate the process of problem solving.

Larkin points out that the problems of mathematics and the physical sciences "are particularly structured domains, tightly organized around a relatively few, broadly applicable principles." On the other hand, the important engineering problems, the solutions to which may make a reputation for the solver, are much less structured; and in many cases, as in the foregoing example, solving the problem begins by finding a way to convert the given situation into a structured one. Many of the problems encountered in science research are also less structured.

In my experience, it has not been as difficult to help students learn to solve problems as it is expensive in time and effort. New problems have to be made up and graded. The grading is a very important activity, because this is where a great deal of the worthwhile coaching occurs. Method must be emphasized; moreover, the result in the best problems is a recommendation or a design rather than a number. These characteristics require more time from the teacher as well as a high level of expertise and so make for expensive teaching. Costs may be held down by using Rubinstein's patterns of course organization. Also Goldstein's coaching computer, when adapted to real-world problems, offers hope of economies.

EXISTING COURSES IN PROBLEM SOLVING

There are courses in problem solving at a number of universities: UCLA, Berkeley, Carnegie-Mellon, and others. The first was described in detail by Rubinstein (1975); there were references by Larkin and Reif to the second; this recapitulation is written from the point of view of one teacher of the third, where the title of the course in engineering, Analysis Synthesis and Evaluation (Neuman, Tuma, Feucht, Paul, & Teare, 1975), translates approximately into "within-paradigm," "new-paradigm," and "third kind" in Scriven's typology. There are other problem-solving courses at Carnegie-Mellon, notably one given in the psychology department by J. R. Hayes.

The teacher cannot but be impressed with the following characteristics of the course Rubinstein described:

1. Its large size.
2. Its nearly even distribution of students among levels, freshmen to senior years.
3. Its wide distribution among majors.
4. Faculty and teaching assistants are drawn from many departments.
5. Such large enrollments and wide diversity require a great deal of organization, and this is provided by Rubinstein. It would be interesting to know more about the content and nature of the training programs.

6. The objectives are pointed toward general problem solving.

7. There is a great deal of flexibility in the course: The teachers may shape their sections according to their own interests, and students may choose some of their assigned problems.

8. There is a fair amount of reading in the course, reading that deals with the heuristics of problem solving, with attitudes and approaches, with specific techniques, with thinking processes, and with problems in the context of human values. Students from diverse backgrounds learn from each other.

9. The course has enjoyed very favorable comments from students and teachers and has stimulated the offering of similar courses at a number of other institutions.

It would be interesting to learn more about the nature of the professional problems that the students deal with in the course, how they deal with them, and how this course improves their performance in later professional courses. In addition, it would be of interest to teachers to know how the UCLA course is related to educational research.

CONCLUSION

In conclusion, what have we teachers learned from this Conference? I think it is the following:

1. On the research side there is still no comprehensive methodology of general problem solving that can be taught and used although considerable progress has been made in the last ten years, based upon detailed observations of the performance of individuals.

2. This has led to the construction of models, some of which have been implemented on the computer. Computers have been programmed to solve problems, many of which have been in the area of puzzles and games, but nevertheless these throw light on the mechanisms of problem solving, and now it seems possible to extend the domains to include real-world problems.

On the teaching side, as Larkin put it, developers of instruction can benefit from what begins to be known about the psychology of problem solving:

1. The student learns to solve problems by solving them.

2. Major emphasis should be placed on method.

3. The teacher is helped in choosing problems by Scriven's typology: "within-paradigm," "new-paradigm," and "third kind." If the student is to reach toward professional standards of problem solving, he/she should have at least some practice in dealing with the latter two types. This probably

means one or more courses directed exclusively to problem solving using the knowledge acquired in previous courses.

4. Rubinstein gives a detailed example of such a course, although it does include new knowledge and techniques, as well as problem solving.

5. In subject matter courses, the student should distinguish between factual and procedural knowledge and learn to put emphasis on the latter.

6. General strategies underlying problem solving (Larkin) include: (a) means–end analysis—where we are, where we want to be, and how to get there; (b) a form of planning—replacing a given difficult situation with a simpler one that retains the central features of the original; after a solution is obtained to the simpler one, it is used as a guide to dealing with the original problem; and (c) a currently unattainable goal is replaced by a subgoal as a step toward achieving the main goal. In dealing with "new-paradigm" problems, the student should also become familiar with the applicable heuristics, especially the importance of understanding the given problem, asking the right questions, thinking out loud and on paper, withholding judgment, using analogous models and diagrams, choosing a principle to start with, selecting suitable coordinates that are explicitly defined, checking results carefully and thoroughly, and finally taking stock to see what has been learned that may be useful in the future.

7. The student should become acquainted with Simon's concept of productions, condition–action pairs, and have practice in using them and in extending his/her own mental file of productions.

Teaching will be made more effective by helping the student learn to utilize these strategies and heuristics and making sure that he/she uses them consciously.

REFERENCES

Neuman, C. P., Tuma, D. T., Feucht, D. L., Paul, F. W., & Teare, B. R. *Analysis, synthesis, and evaluation, adventures in professional engineering problem solving.* Proceedings of the 1975 Conference on Frontiers in Education, Atlanta, Georgia. I. E. E. E. Conference Publication 75CH 1006-6E.

Polya, G. *How to solve it.* Garden City, N.J.: Doubleday, 1952.

Rubinstein, M. F. *Patterns of problem solving.* Englewood Cliffs, N.J.: Prentice-Hall, 1975.

Ver Planck, D. W., & Teare, B. R. *Engineering analysis: An introduction to professional method.* New York: Wiley, 1954.

13 One Final Word

Allen Newell
Carnegie-Mellon University

I was granted the grace of not preparing a substantive paper for this conference on the understanding that I would summarize what has transpired here. The papers and discussions of this conference stand on their own. I am only to package them. That is my task and I need to consider how to do it.

Moshe Rubinstein, in his oral presentation, exhibited the style that has become the hallmark of his own famous course in problem solving. Concerned as much with the involvement, interest, and motivation of the student (here, the audience) as with technical apparatus, he presented us with some simple powerful ideas and encouraged audience participation in identifying them. To pick up where he left off, let me repeat one of his lessons. What is Fig. 13.1?

Good, I see you recognize this to be a tree—a representation that is simple in the extreme but amazingly useful in making sense of a vast array of situations, from organizational structures to games.

Now for the advanced course. *What* in particular does the tree of Fig. 13.1 represent? Following that, how does it help us in our problem? (The reader is invited to try to identify the tree. As in a good detective story, all the information necessary to do so is available.)

Even I admit that the task is a mite difficult. (Though, for all I know, the reader has immediately recognized the tree.) However, in teaching problem solving, one does not simply give the answer, to be ingested passively; rather, one provides hints to encourage more problem solving and involvement. Fig. 13.2 adds some data to our tree. To repeat: What does this tree represent?

At this point there is no alternative to providing the answer. This tree represents the conference. The letters at the nodes are the speakers. Along the

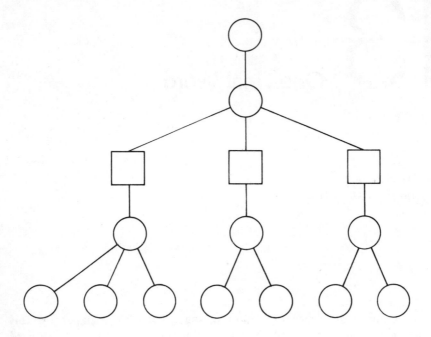

FIG. 13.1. What is this?

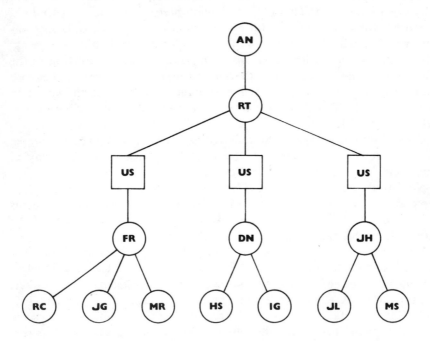

FIG. 13.2. What is this in particular?

bottom are the papers: first President Cyert (RC), then Jim Greno (JG), and Moshe Rubinstein (MR), and so on. These talks are discussed, on the second level, by Fred Reif (RF), Don Norman (DN), and so on; and, above that, in open discussion by all of us (US). The different shaped node (square) indicates that many people talked without preparation, as opposed to the common shape (round), which indicates individually prepared and delivered remarks. At the top there are the final summaries by Richard Teare (RT) and myself (AN).

What can be seen from this representation? We can put to one side the minor insights of the inevitable effect of university presidents on the profound symmetry of academic affairs and the one more bit of evidence for the *principle of self-aggrandizement*—that he who gets to draw the tree puts himself at the top. These are strictly throw-away inferences. More profound is the evidence revealed about the structure of the conference. There was a discussant for each two papers (again, making room for three at the beginning). Furthermore, for each such triple, there was equal time for open discussion. Indeed, this was one of the few conferences in living memory in which there was adequate time to discuss the issues raised by the speakers. Finally, Dick Teare also had the role of discussant of the whole conference. Though theoretically a division of labor existed between Dick Teare and myself—he on practice, me on theory—the distinction is difficult to maintain in reflecting on the important points raised by various papers.

Thus the Conference has had its fill of discussion and summarization, its substance extensively chewed over. This puts my problem in stark relief (always the property of a good representation): What is to be said at this point?

Which reminds me of a story. (Stories are also an arrow in the quiver of the Rubinstein-school of problem-solving education which permits me to retain the story in the written version of these remarks.) The frame story is that at lunch on the first day of the conference, Herb Simon and I were asked by another participant if we remembered a story told at another conference at CMU a few years back about our work in human problem solving, specifically about the book *Human Problem Solving*. Herb didn't remember it, though I did vaguely. That night I checked the proceedings of that conference and found that the discussant had omitted all mention of the story in his written remarks. However, a little forced recall (a technique not much studied by psychologists) finally yielded the story in sufficient detail. Since *Human Problem Solving* has played a modest role in this conference, it is perhaps permissible to tell the story. The original discussant, having chosen to remain silent, will remain nameless.

It seems that *Human Problem Solving* was being used as a textbook in a course on cognitive psychology. The main question on the final examination was "Summarize *Human Problem Solving* in your own words." All of the students immediately began writing, but the instructor noticed that one was simply sitting, staring at the wall. That was all right; as a good student he was no doubt organizing his response. Yet, as the exam passed the half-way point, the student still sat and stared. The instructor could no longer contain himself and he went over to the student. "Don't you understand the question?" "Sure, summarize the text." "Well, didn't you read the text?" "Yes, from cover to cover." "But then surely you can write something." "I can't get started." "Oh come now, we spent all semester on the book; you must have studied it." "I did, I did. But I just can't get started." The instructor was now getting a bit irritated, so he pressed the student on why he couldn't write at least something. "Well," the student explained, "you have to understand how I studied for the examination. I read the whole book carefully and summarized it by writing a single chapter. Then I read that single chapter very carefully and summarized it by writing a page. And then I read that one page ever so carefully and was able to summarize it in a paragraph. And ultimately I summarized that paragraph in a sentence; and that sentence in a single word. Now I can't remember the word, and so I can't get started," "BULLSHIT!" snorted the instructor. "That's it!" cried the student and he started to scribble furiously.

This story, actually, maps onto our tree. You, the readers, have the whole book; each of the primary papers (Greeno, Rubinstein, and on) are a chapter of this book. The discussants (Reif, Norman, and on) should each take a page. Our overall discussion, if we had been as perspicacious as we should have been, should have been a paragraph. Dick Teare should take a sentence and I should find one single final word to characterize the whole conference. It poses my problem in a striking light, as well as illustrating the relatedness of all things, both large and small.

However, all representations and models fail at some point—another lesson all problem solvers must learn. Thus I do not share the opinion of the student. His facile double-four cannot be mine. The topic of this conference is important. The set of researchers who have gathered here to assay where matters stands are a genuinely distinguished group. Indeed, it would be difficult to assemble a more distinguished one. There has been no dearth of issues raised and evidence laid out before us.

My problem is that I am not as talented as that erstwhile student. Perhaps, however, I can find an approximation to his ideal achievement (still one more lesson in general problem solving). A dichotomy is as close to a single word as you can get. Perhaps I can find some dichotomies to express what has been going on at this conference. I have my qualms about dichotomies as the proper form for scientific theories. However, I think dichotomies are fine for conferences. They strip away all the caveats and waffles, focusing the mind on the essential issues.

TABLE 13.1
Dichotomous View of the Conference Papers

R. Cyert	Theory	vs	Heuristics	
J. Greeno	Problem Solving	vs	Knowledge	[False]
M. Rubinstein	Attitude	vs	Technique	
F. Reif	Cog Scientists	vs	Educators	
	Describe		Prescribe	

```
 ┌ ─ ─ ─ ─ ─ ┬ ─ ─ ─ ─ ─ ┐      Computer
 ├ ─ ─ ─ ─ ─ ┼ ─ ─ ─ ─ ─ ┤
 └ ─ ─ ─ ─ ─ ┴ Fourth Quad ┘      Man
```

M. M. Us	Explicit	vs	Tacit	
	Lean	vs	Rich	
I. Goldstein	Technology	vs	Science	
H. Simon	Facts	vs	Access	
D. Norman	Cog Engineering	vs	Cog Science	
M. A. us	External	vs	Internal	
G. Kozmetsky	Generality	vs	Society	
J. Larkin	Lean	vs	Rich	
	Facts	vs	Procedures	
M. Scriven	Describe	vs	Prescribe	
	Theory	vs	Heuristic	
	Paradigm	vs	New	vs Third Kind
J. Hayes	Evaluation	vs	Impression	
T. M. Us	Problem Solving	vs	Knowledge	
	Theory	vs	Heuristic	
	External	vs	Internal	

Thus I herewith present my summarization of the conference in as short a form as is possible for me, one dichotomy per speaker (more or less). (It seems appropriate to omit my fellow summarizer.) I am not sure what to call a collection of dichotomies. Since a good dichotomy should roar like a lion, let me call it a *pride* of dichotomies. Table 13.1 lists them all, to make it easy to keep track. Some of you, especially the speakers, will find this degree of summarization brutal. But that is the way it is with lions, even paper lions.

A PRIDE OF DICHOTOMIES

Cyert: Theory Versus Heuristics. President Cyert provided us with the contrast between a *theory* for how to teach problem solving and having only *heuristic* rules of thumb for doing so. His plea was for us to get some theory to provide some genuine science for the art of teaching. The urgency in his plea was fueled by another dichotomy, that of academia versus change (i.e., that the academy is one of the institutions most resistant to change). But I must discipline myself to minimize the number of dichotomies per person.

Greeno: Problem Solving Versus Knowledge.   Jim focused on the contrast between having the *knowledge* simply to perform a task and having to *problem solve* to obtain a solution. This contrast underlies a great deal of our rhetoric about teaching problem solving—that a student is not to be credited with problem-solving ability if he simply knows how to perform the task. Jim's point was that this dichotomy is false. Modern research in cognitive psychology and artificial intelligence shows that knowledge is at the basis of all problem solving. Our educational task is to discover what knowledge is needed for a class of tasks and then to discover how to communicate that knowledge effectively to our students.

Rubinstein: Attitude Versus Technique.   The *attitudes* of the student toward his problems are as important as the *techniques* that he actually uses to carry out the solution. The term attitudes stands as a symbol for all aspects of a motivational and nonintellective nature. Thus, as noted, Moshe gave us a talk that differed radically from his written text in exemplifying these concerns, seeking to involve us in the basic ideas of his course.

Reif: Cognitive Scientists Versus Educators.   The central theme of Fred Reif's comments is easy enough to state, but it takes three dichotomies to do it. The first is that between *cognitive scientists* and *educators,* which is to be understood as mapping onto the second dichotomy, which is that between *description* of the problem-solving process and *prescription* of it. To convey his special concern, Reif crosses this dichotomy against another one, that between *man* and *computer,* thus generating four cells of societal activity. In three of these cells, the state of the art looks relatively healthy to him. But in the fourth cell, the educator's prescription of how many should learn, things are in a somewhat dismal state. We can call this the *problem of the fourth quad.* It was previewed in Cyert's comments and will show up again. We are not happy with either our present state of scientifically based educational practice or the rapidity of our progress.

Monday Morning Us: Explicit Versus Tacit; Lean Versus Rich.   Two dichotomies emerged during the first morning's discussion. The first was the concern about problem-solving procedures that were *explicit* versus those that were *tacit* or out of awareness. Two themes are possible on this dichotomy: One is a positive concern with how to make problem-solving strategies explicit as communicable principles; the other is a negative concern that certain essential aspects of problem solving remain forever outside of awareness, being learned only by indirection. Hence, we fool ourselves if we focus too strongly on the explicit, and ultimately distort the education of our students. Both attitudes were apparent, if I recall, but the latter was the more urgently pressed. The second dichotomy I have expressed as *lean* problem situations versus *rich* ones. The triggering remarks had to do with problem setting versus problem solving, it being felt that only impoverished, well-defined (i.e., lean) tasks were being considered in which problem solving was sufficient, whereas problem setting, a critical aspect in open, ill-defined (i.e., rich) problematic situations, was being ignored. Both of these dichotomies, explicit versus tacit and rich versus lean, can be seen to have affinities. In part, they jointly reflect the fundamental distrust with the rational that is endemic to the study of human behavior. Whether that distrust is justifiable or not, and whether in the long-term as well as the short-term, remain the open questions. But the lean versus rich dichotomy also reflects the special concern of the conference over whether one can teach problem solving independent of the particular (rich) subject-matter environment.

Goldstein: Technology Versus Science.   We were treated by Ira to a vision of how computer technology could provide an active framework for problem-solving education—in the case at hand, an intelligent tutor in a dynamic game-like learning situation. The issue that emerged for me was whether the primary engine of progress in education was to be *technology,* in providing active and responsive learning environments, or *science,* in providing cognitive theory of how students learn. Many, including Ira I suspect, would maintain this to be a false dichotomy—that you wish to use both engines and there is no reason not to. Be that as it may, Ira's work is in the tradition set by Papert's LOGO project, which eschews finding or verifying new cognitive truths about education but feeds on the novel experiences generated by educational practice in the new technological milieux.

Simon Facts Versus Access.   Herb, as usual, had several things to say. But I want to focus on a single one: It is not sufficient for the student to know just the *facts* that are required for a problem domain; rather, he needs to have *access* to those facts at the right points in problem solving. This is a major corrective to the much-damned view of education as subject matter. It is a positive correction, as opposed to simply asserting that education for problem solving is "more that subject content." The burden of Herb's paper was that research has now told us something about specifying what *access* means in operational terms.

Norman: Cognitive Engineering Versus Cognitive Science.   Don emphasized the nature of a *cognitive engineering* as opposed to a *cognitive science.* They would be different, the former yielding approximate results sufficient unto the day of application thereof. This contrast is clearly of a piece with the concern of Fred Reif and also that of Dick Cyert, though it tries to be more definite about what the appropriate form of cognitive engineering might be.

Monday Afternoon Us: External Versus Internal. There was lots of discussion Monday afternoon, some echoing earlier dichotomies, some new. Letting all else slip away, I retain the issue of whether the student has knowledge for problem solving *externally,* in terms of rules, versus *internally,* in some assimilated and understood form. Research is currently providing explicit rule systems for solving classes of problems, collections of situation–action rules (or production systems), that provide what Herb Simon called for: both access and content. Pragmatically, as cognitive engineers, we think of how to give students such rule systems and, taking the easy road, think of teaching (i.e., telling) them the rules. But then what the student seems to have is an externally formed rule set, and this can be contrasted—shades of Wertheimer—with having a real understanding of how to solve the problems. This dichotomy clearly echoes the morning discussion of *explicit versus tacit* knowledge and *lean versus rich* environments. I enunciate it separately because it found a separate voice in the concern with rule systems.

Kozmetsky: Generality Versus Society. At the banquet,[1] George Kozmetsky, coming not just from a business school but from a background in the systems industry, gave us a dichotomy to ponder distinct from all the others. We researchers talk about problem solving as a *general* capability, useful not only in a subject-matter-free way, but also in a culture-free and society-free way. Our proposals for what is to be taught would apply, we silently aver, to the Lyceum in ancient Greece, the Kpelle of Africa, and the discreet jungles of the modern multinational industrial world. Not to be so sure, was the lesson I took from Kozmetzky (though he said it in positive terms). Each form of *society* (not to speak of different cultures) calls for problem solving of a different kind. Echoing earlier concern for *attitude* over *technique* and what follows from problem solving in *rich* environments rather than *lean* ones, Kozmetsky made the case that basic orientations about what types of problems to pick and how to go about solving them vary with the evolution of society. They are sufficiently basic to be taken as an integral part of the general problem-solving capabilities, not just as added "givens" for specific problems.

---

[1]Some perceptive reader will notice that GK did not make it to the tree of Figure 2. This may be taken as another lesson of the approximate character of representations, or simply as illustrating a sometimes fate of banquet speaker.

Larkin: Lean Versus Rich; Facts Versus Procedures. I have permitted myself two dichotomies for Jill, because both reinforce earlier dichotomies, but with interesting twists. First, Jill emphasized the distinction between *lean* tasks, such as laboratory puzzle solving, and *rich* tasks, such as physics problems. But contrary to the flavor of the earlier remarks, she felt that research was now moving into these richer areas and was finding that it could cope with the added complexity. Furthermore, her analysis showed the ingredients in these rich environments to be part of the same cognitive story that has emerged from the leaner tasks. This can be captured in the distinction between just having the *facts* of physics and having *procedures* for solving the problems. This is the same distinction of *facts* versus *access* that I laid at Herb Simon's door, extended to talk more about the total strategies of use.

Scriven: Describe Versus Prescribe; Theory Versus Heuristic; Paradigm Versus New Versus Third Kind. All philosophers confound (Scriven is a philosopher; therefore, Scriven confounds). In part, Michael's talk emphasized dichotomies with which we have already become familiar. One was the distinction between *description* and *prescription,* where he came down foursquare for more status for prescription, thus joining Fred Reif and others as well. Another was the dichotomy between *theory* and *heuristic,* where, contra Dick Cyert, he allowed as how no theory in the usual sense might be possible. We might be stuck with simply having odd rules of thumb. The center of his talk was what confounded me (not his audience). He introduced a class of problems, which he called *problems of the third kind,* and it is beyond me how to characterize this as a dichotomy. The first two kinds, *paradigm* and *new,* correspond roughly to having knowledge of how to solve the problem and not having that knowledge—namely, to the distinction made and declared false by Jim Greeno. No matter; the important point for Scriven was the existence of the third kind. Although he gave no clean formulation, it appears from his examples and discussion that these are rich problems in which the evaluation is problematical, hence it becomes the focus of the problem-solving activity.

Hayes: Evaluation Versus Impressions. In his discussion, Dick introduced a distinction that I think was needed—that between deliberate *evaluation* of our attempts to teach problem solving and being satisfied with informal *impressions* of whether we are having an effect. I have balked at using the term *formal evaluation,* because in current educational practice that connotes a rather specific enterprise. But the issue remains. Of course, Moshe Rubinstein's course is successful. Look at all the usual measures: longevity, student testimonials, student demand, copying, being called to conferences to talk about the course. Most of us settle for far, far less. Yet we don't know much about whether the students really learn general problem-solving skills. I welcomed the evidence Moshe quoted using the intelligence test, though I shared Dick Hayes' concerns.

Tuesday Morning Us: Problem Solving Versus Knowledge; Theory Versus Heuristic; External Versus Internal.   For my money, our final morning of discussion distributed attention on issues already set. Could there be *problem solving* independent of the *knowledge* of specific domains? Could there be a *theory* of problem solving actually useful to practice, or only *heuristics.* And did the sorts of information that current research yielded, which seemed to be *external* rules, touch the kinds of *internal* knowledge that successful problem solvers seem to have?

CAN GENERAL PROBLEM SOLVING BE TAUGHT?

Table 13.1 is still a whole page fulll of dichotomies. Perhaps, if written end to end, they would compress to a paragraph. However, this remains a far cry from the accomplishments of our mythical student.

Let me take my stand then. If there was one dichotomy that permeated this conference, it concerned the basic nature of problem solving. Specifically, the poles are:

Domain-independence   vs   Domain-specificity
of Problem Solving   of Problem Solving

The dichotomy is an old one. As Herb Simon noted, the issue once was whether students should be taught Latin in order to improve their minds, which is to say, to give them general problem-solving skills. The prescientific (i.e., pre-experimental psychology) position was: Of course, you trained the mind to discipline. The answer of Thorndike was that Latin didn't help a bit. There has followed a long history of failure to find appreciable transfer from training on one task to success on another. The modern (i.e., experimental psychology) position is that learned problem-solving skills are, in general, idiosyncratic to the task.[2]

The participants at this conference have a large investment in this dichotomy. Many of us are involved in the design and implementation of courses that teach people how to problem solve. This enterprise is truly quixotic, if problem solving cannot be divorced from specific subject-matter

---

[2]This is not negated by the equally long history, in intelligence testing, of finding a general factor (G), so that people who are good at solving one task tend to be good at solving many other tasks—at least as long as intelligence is assumed to be genetic or (more weakly) not teachable.

content. We keep alive the faith of the Latin teachers. But our stock in trade is the modern elements of abstraction, mathematics, and heuristics. Instead of Latin, we teach about abstract trees, probability theory, and the guidelines of Polya. Moshe Rubinstein's course and the engineering analysis courses taught here at CMU for so long (as Dick Teare brought out) stand as exemplars. In addition, modern information-processing theories of human problem-solving have a decidedly general ring. Almost automatically, this theory seems to imply teaching general problem solving. The conference repeatedly talked about "means-ends analysis" as a general method that subjects employed successfully. Hence, it seems we should add the teaching of these methods to the other elements of our course in general problem solving.

Both these investments tilt toward the pole of finding that problem solving is sufficiently independent of domain so that a scientific basis exists for teaching problem solving. But many here are also mindful of the history of limited results on transfer of learning. Also, as Jim Greeno maintained, grounds exist within current research for leaning toward the more specific pole. Thus a fair summary says the conference saw this basic dichotomy as unresolved.

In my view, considerable advance has taken place in our understanding, despite the lack of resolution. Research, much of it represented here at this conference, has made concrete the possible operational structures that can underly general problem solving. These several possibilities are not all mutually exclusive. More important, they have different implications for the teachability of general problem-solving skills, both whether it is possible and how it should be conducted. Many of these mechanisms were discussed in one way or another during the conference. However, no one had occasion to bring them all together. Let me enumerate them here briefly, because an overview is important to assessing where we stand on our ultimate dichotomy.

Big Switch. The problem solver consists of a very large number of highly specific procedures, akin to current application programs in their specificity, with a discrimination net (the big switch) for getting access to them. Tens of thousands of such procedures form a mosaic that covers the world of all tasks. Each procedure has a small penumbra of generality, so that in total a large area of novel tasks can be accomplished.

Big Memory. This is a variant of the Big Switch theory with the emphasis on the web of facts rather than on their procedural character. It is the classic subject-matter-is-all hypothesis. It presumes some way of putting the facts together but is silent on what that is. On the other hand, its modern version includes the notion that the accessing structure is as important as the facts themselves.

TABLE 13.2
The Main Weak Methods

GT: Generate and Test.   The simplest method of all. Solution candidates are generated one by one and tested to see if acceptable.

HC: Hill Climbing.   If a graded evaluation function exists, then one can search locally for steps that move one continually to higher values.

HS: Heuristic Search.   A set of basic operators that can be used to search in a problem space. Requires memory to keep prior positions in the space so that search can backtrack and continue in different directions.

MEA: Means-Ends Analysis.   A variant of Heuristic Search where enough knowledge is available about the goal states to (1) diagnose the difference between it and the present position, and (2) use that difference to determine which operator to apply.

OSG: Operator Subgoaling.   If an operator is attempted and fails, then one can set up a subgoal of changing the situation to make the operator applicable. Shows up almost universally with MEA but is an independent method.

SGD: Subgoal Decomposition.   Decompose the task into a set of subtasks, each of which does part of the total job, hence all (or most) of which must be accomplished. Each subtask is presumably easier in some way than the original. (Often called Divide and Conquer.)

MCH: Match.   If one has a schematic form for the solution, bring the form into correspondence with the situation, step by step, to determine the missing (variable) elements of the form.

HMCH: Hypothesize and Match: Generate and Test on a space of schematic hypotheses; then match to the situation to instantiate a hypothesis that fits. Using schematic, rather than totally specified, hypotheses keeps the generation to tolerable levels.

CS: Constraint Satisfaction.   Given a set of constraints convert each constraint into either part of a generator (preferably) or part of a test, and solve the problem by Generate and Test.

Weak Methods.   There are a set of highly general methods that constitute the core of general problem solving. These are called *weak*, because they trade generality for power. Each differs slightly in what it assumes known about the problem. Table 13.2 lists the most well known of these weak methods. They have been established mostly from work in artificial intelligence, but can be found in psychological studies as well.

Weak to Strong Method Sequence.   The weak methods can be taken to be just the tip of the iceberg, so that there exists an expanding cone of methods of ever greater specificity and power. This is a variant of the Big Switch hypothesis, for at the base of the cone are the multitude of specific expert procedures. Yet the apex of the cone provides the general ways of responding to tasks that are quite different from any for which the problem solver could have developed expert procedures.

Mapping.   Generality arises from the ability of the problem solver to map the situation he faces into something he knows. Simple maps look like matches to symbolic forms. But more complex mappings are common, some of which we call *analogy* and *metaphor*. At least two branches exist: (1)

concrete methods developed for other tasks become candidate methods for the given task, so the problem solver always has a repertoire of methods available; in the limit there never exist "general methods," because one always analogizes from some concrete methods; (2) general ideas ("Debug your plan," "Treat it like an energy-conservation problem") can be mapped into concrete situations so as actually to guide behavior.

Planning.   The problem solver first constructs a plan in some abstract or simplified space and then uses the plan as a guide to solving the problem. By abstraction, one can always get to a sufficiently simplified situation to be able to solve the problem by relatively simple means (e.g., the weak methods, or because it is familiar and you have expert procedures in the simplified situation).

Learning.   Generality is located not in the ability to perform but in the ability to learn. In a hard problem, the problem solver must actually learn the pieces out of which a solution is to be fashioned. Search becomes not so much to solve a problem as to learn about the domain.

Discipline.   It should never be forgotten that the source of the ability to solve problems may lie outside of the cognitive world entirely, being related instead to the ability to manage intellectual resources—to devote attention to the task, to actually carry through mental calculations. All this I have simply summarized in the term *discipline.*

I do not take the trouble to identify carefully all those who mentioned, discussed, and disputed these different mechanisms during the conference. Several of our dichotomies comment directly on aspects of these mechanisms: problem-solving versus knowledge, facts versus access, facts versus procedures, and attitude versus technique. Nor did I mean to provide more complete or better statements than those given during the conference. I only wished to evoke them all in one place. I did list several weak methods, because it seemed to me that the conference slipped into the habit of talking mostly about means-ends analysis.

Our ultimate dichotomy involves not just the nature of general problem solving but whether it can be taught independently of specific subject matter. The mechanisms just listed give a range of different answers. The Big Switch and Big Memory represent the denial of the ability to teach problem solving independently. The Weak Methods offers the clearest basis for doing it. But Planning, Mapping, and Learning also hold out potential, if somewhat different, bases. Each of these holds the promise that it could indeed be a separable general skill that could be taught [e.g., one could learn how to go about mapping the actual situation into some recalled situation, and this skill—the method of mapping—would be a prime determiner of the success rather than, say, the chance of retrieving an appropriate situation from memory]. Ditto with learning: It could have some uniform characteristics [e.g., observation, comparison with requirements, devotion of sufficient attention to assure retention] that could be taught separately and thus would enhance problem solving generally.

From what we now know, all these mechanisms seem likely to play some role in attaining generality in problem solving, though we are unable yet to assess their relative importance. Without such an assessment, it is difficult to state with confidence where the effort should go in teaching general problem-solving ability—or to determine the extent to which it is possible. However, having mechanistic formulations of these alternatives at hand, each having been instantiated in studies in cognitive psychology and artificial intelligence, constitutes important progress. We can expect gradual and steady clarification of the role of these mechanisms in generality.

With respect to teaching, all the bases for generality—weak methods, planning, mapping and learning—have one thing in common. They all involve mechanisms of great generality (which is why they are useful as a basis for generality, to speak an almost tautology). Hence, they require that we can teach students such general mechanisms. There is considerable lore on whether this can be done (e.g., that you have to let students learn it by experience). However, there seems to be little in the way of science about the issue. A few good experimental–theoretical forays into the information processes that go on when a student must learn a highly abstract principle and then apply it in several different situations—say in the style of Hayes and Simon's work on assimilating new problems—would do wonders for our understanding of this issue.

Another important issue about learning is raised by the external versus internal dichotomy. Information-processing analyses, when well done, produce explicit formulations of rule systems. In the case at hand, we can produce rule systems for dealing with mapping, weak methods, or any of the other bases for generality. With further search such formulations might acquire sufficient generality to approximate what students need to learn in a course on general problem solving. The conference exhibited considerable confusions about the status of such rules. If we wish a person to acquire such a rule system, does he first learn it as a verbal formula, which he then consults as if it were a text from a Chinese fortune cookie? As far as I could detect, the concern with external rules versus internal understanding was saturated with such worries. To express it as I have, of course, is already to half dissolve the issue. But some important reality remains.

One clear fact of psychology is that of automatization. With experience or practice, performance on tasks speeds up, shapes up, and involves decreased awareness, however measured. The phenomena is ubiquitous, showing up in all types of tasks: motor, sensory, and intellectual (or cognitive). The evidence in the literature is overwhelming (much data from learning curves, simultaneous tasking, etc.), and there are a few ideas (e.g., the tests drop out). But, in fact, we really are still basically at sea about the phenomena, with no adequate characterization.

This is the phenomena that feeds the external–internal dichotomy. When we first learn things, they are in a different form (mostly) from how they are after further experience (automatization? assimilation? integration? choose your own word). Currently, the rule systems we cognitive scientists create to describe our subjects are fundamentally neutral on which internal organizations they reflect. They do not necessarily reflect only a verbal (Chinese fortune cookie) level. But they are essentially silent on the question. Without some theoretical and experimental clarity on this issue we find it hard to avoid being as confused as our internal–external dichotomy revealed us to be. More important, we find it hard to make progress on whether it is possible to teach highly general methods and to discover the right ways to do it.

CONCLUSION

I trust it is evident that I stand with the optimists. A cognitive science is not only possible but is happening. It can engender and support a cognitive engineering (in Don Norman's phrase), useful for teaching students how to think, among other things. In due time, it will dissolve many of the dichotomies I have so carefully extracted. It certainly should do so for the basic issue that has remained with us throughout: whether one can teach general problem-solving skills. That I conclude by calling for additional research to promote that dissolution indicates that there is no final word.

APPENDIXES

APPENDICES

List of Contributors

Richard M. Cyert
    President, Carnegie-Mellon University, Pittsburgh, Pa. 15213

Ira Goldstein
    Artificial Intelligence Laboratory, Massachusetts Institute of Technology, Cambridge, Mass. 02139. (Present affiliation: Xerox Research Center, 3333 Coyote Hill Road, Palo Alto, Calif. 94304)

James G. Greeno
    Learning Research and Development Center, University of Pittsburgh, Pittsburgh, Pa. 15260

John R. Hayes
    Department of Psychology, Carnegie-Mellon University, Pittsburgh, Pa. 15213

George Kozmetsky
    Graduate School of Business, University of Texas, Austin, Tex. 78712

Jill H. Larkin
    Group in Science and Mathematics Education, University of California, Berkeley, 94720. (Present affiliation: Department of Psychology, Carnegie-Mellon University, Pittsburgh, Pa. 15213)

Allen Newell
    Department of Computer Science, Carnegie-Mellon University, Pittsburgh, Pa. 15213

Donald Norman
    Department of Psychology, University of California at San Diego, La Jolla, Calif. 92093

Frederick Reif
   Department of Physics and Group in Science and Mathematics Education, University of California, Berkeley, Calif. 94720

Moshe Rubinstein
   Department of Engineering Systems, University of California, Los Angeles, Calif. 90024

Michael Scriven
   School of Education, University of San Francisco, San Francisco, Calif. 94117

Herbert A. Simon
   Department of Psychology, Carnegie-Mellon University, Pittsburgh, Pa. 15213

B. Richard Teare
   Carnegie Institute of Technology, Carnegie-Mellon University, Pittsburgh, Pa. 15213

Conference Participants

Royal G. Albridge
Vanderbilt University
Box 1815, Station B
Nashville, Tenn. 37235

Joseph Ballay
Design Department
Carnegie-Mellon University
5000 Forbes Avenue
Pittsburgh, Pa. 15213

Robert Baum
Human Dimension Center
Rensselaer Polytechnic Inst.
Troy, N. Y. 12181

Robert Bauman
Dept. of Physics
University of Alabama
Birmingham, Ala. 35294

Daniel Berg
Dean, MIS
Carnegie-Mellon University
5000 Forbes Avenue
Pittsburgh, Pa. 15213

J. Anthony Blair
Department of Philosophy
University of Windsor
Windsor, Ontario N9B 3P4
Canada

John Seely Brown
Xerox Research Center
3333 Coyote Hill Road
Palo Alto, Calif. 94304

Robert Carlin
Chemistry Dept.
Carnegie-Mellon University
5000 Forbes Avenue
Pittsburgh, Pa. 15213

Stanley Charap
Electrical Engineering
Carnegie-Mellon University
5000 Forbes Avenue
Pittsburgh, Pa. 15213

Susan F. Chipman
National Institute of Education
1200 19th St., N.W.
Washington, D.C. 20208

John Clement
Cognitive Department Project
Physics Dept.
University of Massachusetts
Amherst, Mass. 01003

Jan Cohn
English Department
Carnegie-Mellon University
5000 Forbes Avenue
Pittsburgh, Pa. 15213

Preston Covey
History and Philosophy Dept.
Carnegie-Mellon University
5000 Forbes Avenue
Pittsburgh, Pa. 15213

John P. Crecine
Dean, H&SS
Carnegie-Mellon University
5000 Forbes Avenue
Pittsburgh, Pa. 15213

Richard Cyert
President
Carnegie-Mellon University
5000 Forbes Avenue
Pittsburgh, Pa. 15213

Gene D'Amour
Philosophy Dept.
West Virginia University
Morgantown, W. Va. 26506

Robert B. Davis
University of Illinois
603 West Michigan Avenue
Urbana, Ill. 61801

Andrea A. diSessa
MIT DSRE
MIT 20C-105
Cambridge, Mass. 02139

Charles Eastman
SUPA
Carnegie-Mellon University
5000 Forbes Avenue
Pittsburgh, Pa. 15213

Marshall J. Farr
Personnel and Training
   Research Programs
Office of Naval Research
Arlington, Va. 22217

Steven Fenves
Civil Engineering
Carnegie-Mellon University
5000 Forbes Avenue
Pittsburgh, Pa. 15213

Gerhard Fischer
MIT AI Lab
Room 340
545 Technology Square
Cambridge, Mass. 02139

George Fix
Dept. of Mathematics
Carnegie-Mellon University
5000 Forbes Avenue
Pittsburgh, Pa. 15213

Linda Flower
GSIA
Carnegie-Mellon University
5000 Forbes Avenue
Pittsburgh, Pa. 15213

Edward A. Friedman
Dean of the College
Stevens Institute of Technology
Hoboken, N.J. 07030

Maynard Fuller
Chemical Engineering Dept.
McGill University
3480 University Street
Montreal, Quebec H3A 2A7
Canada

Mary Gick
Psychology Dept.
University of Michigan
330 Packard Road
Ann Arbor, Mich. 48104

Adele Goldberg
Xerox Research Center
3333 Coyote Hill Road
Palo Alto, Calif. 94304

Ira Goldstein
Xerox Research Center
3333 Coyote Hill Road
Palo Alto, Calif. 94304

Lois B. Greenfield
College of Engineering
T-24
University of Wisconsin
Madison, Wis. 53706

James G. Greeno
801 LRDC Building
University of Pittsburgh
3939 O'Hara Street
Pittsburgh, Pa. 15260

Henry M. Halff
Assistant Director
Personnel and Training
  Research Programs
Office of Naval Research
Arlington, Va. 22217

John R. Hayes
Psychology Dept.
Carnegie-Mellon University
5000 Forbes Avenue
Pittsburgh, Pa. 15213

Keith Holyoak
Dept. of Psychology
University of Michigan
330 Packard Road
Ann Arbor, Mich. 48104

Julia S. Hough
The Franklin Institute Press
20th and Race Streets
Philadelphia, Pa. 19103

Alice M. Isen
American Psychological Association
1200 17th St., N.W.
Washington, D.C. 20036

Robert Kaplan
GSIA
Carnegie-Mellon University
5000 Forbes Avenue
Pittsburgh, Pa. 15213

James J. Kaput
Dept. of Mathematics
Southeastern Massachusetts University
No. Dartmouth, Mass. 02747

Alan Kay
Xerox Corporation
Palo Alto Research Center
3333 Coyote Hill Road
Palo Alto, Calif. 94025

David Klahr
Psychology Dept.
Carnegie Mellon University
5000 Forbes Avenue
Pittsburgh, Pa. 15213

Kenneth Kortanek
Dept. of Mathematics
Carnegie-Mellon University
5000 Forbes Avenue
Pittsburgh, Pa. 15213

George Kozmetsky
Graduate School of Business
University of Texas at Austin
Austin, Tex. 78712

Lev Landa
Center for Educational Experience,
Development, and Evaluation
University of Iowa
218 Lindguist Center
Iowa City, Iowa. 52242

Jill H. Larkin
Psychology Dept.
Carnegie-Mellon University
5000 Forbes Avenue
Pittsburgh, Pa. 15213

Joseph I. Lipson
National Science Foundation
SEDAR W-638
5225 Wisconsin Avenue, N.W.
Washington, D.C. 20550

Jack Lochhead
Physics Dept.
University of Massachusetts
Amherst, Mass. 01003

Marilyn Matz
Bolt, Beranek and Newman, Inc.
50 Moulton Street
Cambridge, Mass. 02138

Michael A. McDanield
Division of Institutes and
Manager Development
Rider Course
P.O. Box 6400
Lawrenceville, N.J. 08648

Curtis C. McKnight
Curriculum Lab
University of Illinois
1212 W. Springfield
Urbana, Ill. 61801

Erik D. McWilliams
SEDAR Division
National Science Foundation
1800 G Street, N.W.
Washington, D.C. 20050

Gerald Nadler
Dept. of Industrial Engineering
University of Wisconsin-Madison
1513 University Avenue
Madison, Wis. 53706

Carl Naegele
Science and Math Teaching Center
Michigan State University
East Lansing, Mich. 48824

Allen Newell
Computer Science Dept.
Carnegie-Mellon University
5000 Forbes Avenue
Pittsburgh, Pa. 15213

Donald Norman
Dept. of Psychology
University of California at San Diego
LaJolla, Calif. 92093

Kathleen O'Brien
Alverno College
3401 S. 39th Street
Milwaukee, Wis. 53215

Helen L. Plants
College of Engineering
West Virginia University
Morgantown, W. Va. 26506

Alexander Pollatsek
Dept. of Psychology
University of Massachusetts
Amherst, Mass. 01003

Frederick Reif
Physics Dept.
University of California
Berkeley, Calif. 94720

Lauren Resnick
LRDC Building
University of Pittsburgh
3939 O'Hara Street
Pittsburgh, Pa. 15260

James Romualdi
Civil Engineering
Carnegie-Mellon University
5000 Forbes Avenue
Pittsburgh, Pa. 15213

Mary Budd Rowe
Research in Science Education
National Science Foundation
Washington, D.C. 20550

Moshe Rubinstein
Engineering Systems Dept.
University of California
Los Angeles, Calif. 90024

Joseph M. Scandura
Learning Center
University of Pennsylvania
3700 Walnut Street
Philadelphia, Pa. 19104

Edward Schatz
Vice President of
Academic Affairs
Carnegie-Mellon University
5000 Forbes Avenue
Pittsburgh, Pa. 15213

Charles F. Schmidt
Dept. of Psychology
Rutgers University
New Brunswick, N.J. 08903

Alan H. Schoenfeld
Department of Mathematics
Hamilton College
Clinton, N.Y. 13323

Thomas Schwartz
Dept. of Government
University of Texas at Austin
Austin, Tex. 78712

Michael Scriven
School of Education
University of San Francisco
Golden Gate & Parker Avenue
San Francisco, Calif. 94117

John T. Sears
Dept. of Chemical Engineering
West Virginia University
Morgantown, W. Virginia. 26506

Robert Sekerka
Metallurgy and Materials Science
Carnegie-Mellon University
5000 Forbes Avenue
Pittsburgh, Pa. 15213

Herbert Simon
Dept. of Psychology
Carnegie-Mellon University
5000 Forbes Avenue
Pittsburgh, Pa. 15213

Edward L. Smith
Science & Math Teaching Center
E-37 McDonel Hall
Michigan State University
East Lansing, Mich. 48824

Elliot M. Soloway
Computer and Information Science
University of Massachusetts
Amherst, Mass. 01003

Sarah Sprafka
OMERAD
A-214 East Fee Hall
Michigan State University
East Lansing, Mich. 48824

Esther R. Steinberg
252 Engineering Research Lab
Urbana, Ill. 61801

Lawrence M. Stolurow
Center for Education Experience,
Development, and Evaluation
University of Iowa
218 Lindguist Center
Iowa City, 52242

B. Richard Teare
Dean, CIT
Carnegie-Mellon University
5000 Forbes Avenue
Pittsburgh, Pa. 15213

Herbert Toor
Dean, CIT
Carnegie-Mellon University
5000 Forbes Avenue
Pittsburgh, Pa. 15213

David T. Tuma
Electrical Engineering
Carnegie-Mellon University
5000 Forbes Avenue
Pittsburgh, Pa. 15213

Kurt VanLehn
Bolt, Beranek, and Newman, Inc.
50 Moulton Street
Cambridge, Mass. 02138

Roger Volkema
2329 Monroe Street
Madison, Wis. 53711

Arnold D. Well
Dept. of Psychology
University of Massachusetts
Amherst, Mass. 01003

Richard A. Wertime
Dept. of English
104 Classroom Building
Beaver College
Glenside, Pa. 19046

Keith T. Wescourt
Assistant Director
Personnel & Training
   Research Programs
Office of Naval Research
800 N. Quincy Street
Arlington, Va. 22217

Donald R. Woods
Chemical Engineering
McMaster University
Hamilton, Ontario L8S 4L7
Canada

Jay Yellen
Dept. of Math
SUNY
College of Fredonia
Fredonia, N.Y. 14063

Hugh Young
Physics Dept.
Carnegie-Mellon University
5000 Forbes Avenue
Pittsburgh, Pa. 15213

Richard Young
English Dept.
Carnegie-Mellon University
5000 Forbes Avenue
Pittsburgh, Pa. 15213

Leon W. Zelby
School of EE & Comp. Sci.
University of Oklahoma
202 W. Boyd Street
Norman, Ok. 73019

Selected Bibliography

To help readers of these Proceedings to gain greater familiarity with the literature relevant to problem solving, several conference participants suggested references that might be useful. The resulting list of references, appended below, is not intended to be complete, but should serve as a useful guide.

BASIC ISSUES AND APPROACHES

Anderson, R. C., Spiro, R. J., & Montague, W. E. (Eds.). *Processes in acquiring knowledge.* Hillsdale, N.J.: Lawrence Erlbaum Associates, 1976.

Bhaskar, R., & Simon, H. A. Problem solving in semantically rich domains: An example from engineering thermodynamics. *Cognitive Science,* 1977, *1,* 193–215.

Boden, M. A. *Artificial intelligence and natural man.* New York: Basic Books, 1977.

Brown, J. S., & Burton, R. R. Diagnostic models for procedural bugs in basic mathematical skills. *Cognitive Science,* 1978, *2,* 155–192.

Brown, J. S., Collins, A., & Harris, G. Artificial intelligence and learning strategies. In H. O'Neil, *Learning strategies.* New York: Academic Press, 1978.

Davis, G. A. *Psychology of problem solving.* New York: Basic Books, 1973.

Greeno, J. G. Indefinite goals in well-structured problems. *Psychological Review,* 1976, *83,* 479–491.

Hayes, J. R. *Cognitive psychology: Thinking and creativity.* Homewood, Ill.: Dorsey Press, 1978.

Hayes, J. R., & Simon, H. A. Understanding written problem instructions. In L. W. Gregg (Ed.), *Knowledge and cognition.* Hillsdale, N.J.: Lawrence Erlbaum Associates, 1974.

Kilpatrick, J., & Wirszup, I. (Eds.). *Soviet studies in the psychology of learning and teaching mathematics* (Vols. 3, 4, and 6). Chicago: University of Chicago, 1969, 1970, 1972.

Klahr, D. (Ed.). *Cognition and instruction.* Hillsdale, N.J.: Lawrence Erlbaum Associates, 1976.

Klahr, D., & Siegler, R. S. *The representation of children's knowledge. In H. Reese & L. P. Lipsitt (Eds.), Advances in child development.* New York: Academic Press, 1977.

Kleinmuntz, B. (Ed.). *Problem solving: Research, method, and theory.* New York: Wiley, 1966.

Larkin, J. H., & Reif, F. Understanding and teaching problem solving in physics. *European Journal of Science Education,* 1979, *1,* 191–203.

Mayer, R. E. *Thinking and problem solving: An introduction to human cognition and learning.* Glenview, Ill.: Scott, Foresman, 1977.

Newell, A., & Simon, H. A. *Human problem solving.* Englewood Cliffs, N.J.: Prentice-Hall, 1972.

Pople, H. Problem solving: An exercise in synthetic reasoning. *International Joint Conference on Artificial Intelligence,* 1977, *5,* 1030–1037.

Posner, M. I. *Cognition: An introduction* (Chap. 7). Glenview, Ill.: Scott, Foresman, 1973.

Raphael, B. *The thinking computer: Mind inside matter.* San Francisco: Freeman, 1976.

Resnick, L. B. (Ed.). *The nature of intelligence.* Hillsdale, N.J.: Lawrence Erlbaum Associates, 1976.

Sacerdoti, E. *A structure for plans and behavior.* New York: Elsevier North-Holland, 1977.

Scandura, J. M. *Problem solving: A structural/process approach with instructional implications.* New York: Academic Press, 1977.

Simon, D. P., & Simon, H. A. Individual differences in solving physics problems. In R. Siegler (Ed.), *Children's thinking: What develops?* Hillsdale, N.J.: Lawrence Erlbaum Associates, 1978.

Simon, H. A., & Hayes, J. R. The understanding process: Problem isomorphs. *Cognitive Psychology,* 1976, *8,* 165–194.

Wertheimer, M. *Productive thinking* (enlarged ed.). New York: Harper & Row, 1959.

Winston, P. H. *Artificial intelligence.* Reading, Mass.: Addison Wesley, 1977.

INSTRUCTION IN PROBLEM-SOLVING SKILLS

Adams, J. L. *Conceptual blockbusting.* San Francisco: Freeman, 1974.

Black, M. *Critical thinking.* Englewood Cliffs, N.J.: Prentice-Hall, 1946.

de Bono, E. *Lateral thinking: Creativity step by step.* New York: Harper & Row, 1970.

Landa, L. N. *Algorithmization in learning and instruction.* Englewood Cliffs, N.J: Educational Technology Publicatins, 1974.

Landa, L. N. *Instructional regulation and control.* Englewood Cliffs, N.J.: Educational Technology Publications, 1976.

Lochhead, J., & Clement, J. (Eds.). *Cognitive-process instruction.* Philadelphia, Pa.: Franklin Institute Press, 1979.

Lubkin, J. (Ed.). *The teaching of elementary problem solving in engineering and related fields.* Washington, D. C.: American Society for Engineering Education (1 Dupont Circle, Washington, D. C. 20036), 1979.

Maier, N. R. F. *Problem solving and creativity in individuals and groups.* Belmont, Calif.: Wadsworth Publ. Co., 1970.

McKim, R. H. *Experiences in visual thinking.* Monterey, Calif.: Brooks/Cole, 1972.

Papert, S. M. Teaching children to be mathematicians versus teaching about mathematics. *International Journal of Mathematical Education in Science and Technology,* 1972, *3,* 249–262.

Parnes, S. J. *Creative behavior guidebook.* New York: Scribner's 1967.

Polya, G. *How to solve it* (2nd ed.). Garden City, N. Y.: Doubleday, 1957.

Reif, F. Problem solving in physics or engineering: Human information processing and some teaching suggestions. In J. Lubkin (Ed.), *The teaching of elementary problem solving in engineering and related fields.* Washington, D. C.: American Society for Engineering Education, 1979.

Reif, F., Larkin, J. H., & Brackett, G. B. Teaching general learning and problem-solving skills. *American Journal of Physics,* 1976, *44,* 212-217.

Rubinstein, M. F. *Patterns of problem solving.* Englewood Cliffs, N.J.: Prentice-Hall, 1974.

Schoenfeld, A. H. Can heuristics be taught?. In J. Lochhead & J. Clement (Eds.), *Cognitive process instruction.* Philadelphia, Pa.: Franklin Institute Press, 1979.

Upton, A., & Samson, R. W. *Creative analysis.* New York: Dutton, 1961.

Warren, T. F., & Davis, G. A. Techniques for creative thinking: An empirical comparison of three methods. *Psychological Reports,* 1969, *25,* 207-214.

Whimbey, A., & Whimbey, L. *Intelligence can be taught.* Stamford, Conn.: Innovative Sciences, 1978.

Wickelgren, W. A. *How to solve problems.* San Francisco: Freeman, 1973.

PROBLEM SOLVING IN ENGINEERING

Krick, E. *An introduction to engineering methods, concepts, and issues.* New York: Wiley, 1976.

Neuman, C. P., Tuma, D. T., Feucht, D. L., Paul, F. W., & Teare, B. R. Analysis, synthesis, and evaluation: Adventures in professional engineering problem solving. *Proceedings of the Frontiers in Education ASEE/IEEE Conference,* October 1975.

Russel, F., & Dean, M. *Introduction to chemical engineering analysis.* New York: Wiley, 1972.

Ver Planck, D. W., & Teare, B. R. *Engineering analysis.* New York: Wiley, 1954.

Woods, D. R. *Survey of ideas for teaching problem solving.* (Tech. Rep.). Hamilton, Ontario, Canada: Department of Chemical Engineering, McMaster University, 1976.

Woodson, T. T. *Introduction to engineering design.* New York: McGraw-Hill, 1966.

Author Index

Numbers in italic indicate the page on which the complete reference appears.

A

Abelson, R., 117, *124*
Adams, J. L., *202*
Anderson, R. C., *201*
Anzai, Y., 90, *95*
Arkin, F., 101, *107*
Atwood, M. E., 14, 22

B

Bagnall, J., 142, *147*
Bauman, R. P., 112, *124*
Bell, A., 56, *78*
Bhaskar, R., *201*
Black, M., *202*
Bloom, B., 112, *124*
Bobrow, D. G., 16, *22,* 74, *79*
Boden, M. A., *201*
Bott, R., 105, *107*
Brackett, G. B., *203*
Broder, L., 112, *124*
Brown, J. S., 56, 57, 67, *78, 201*
Burton, R., 56, 57, 67, *78*

C

Carbonell, J., 56, *79*
Carr, B., 56, 60, *79*
Chase, W. G., 15, *22*
Clancey, W. B., 56, *79*
Clement, J., *202*
Collins, A., 120, *124, 201*

D

Davis, G. A., *201, 203*
Davis, R., 76, *79*
Dean, M., *203*
de Bono, E., *202*
de Kleer, J., 16, *22,* 122, *124*

E

Erickson, 138, *139*

205

Subject Index